TREATISE

ON

PHYSICAL EDUCATION,

FOUNDED ON

PHYSIOLOGICAL PRINCIPLES;

AND UNDER THE

IMMEDIATE PATRONAGE   FACULTY.

BY

LOUIS HUGUENIN,

PROFESSOR OF GYMNASTICS, LIVERPOOL.

MEMBER'S ANNUAL SUBSCRIPTION, ONE GUINEA. *(left margin)*

LADY'S ANNUAL SUBSCRIPTION, HALF A GUINEA. *(right margin)*

TERMS.

The Fees are £8 per Annum to Sons of Members, payable in advance at the following dates, and in the following sums:—

1st May.	1st August.	1st November.	1st. February.
9s.	17s.	17s.	17s.

Other Pupils pay 10s. additional per Annum.

These Fees include a charge of 10s. per Annum for the Books, Slates, Copy Books, &c., used in School, which are supplied by the Institution. Chemicals are charged for, at the rate of 1s. per Quarter, and Drawing Books, Pencils, &c., according to the consumption.

There are at present several vacancies for Pupils as Normal Teachers.

2. HIGH SCHOOL.

Dr. IHNE, lately Classical Master in the Royal Protestant Gymnasium at Elberfeld, Prussia, Author of "Researches Concerning the Development of the Roman Constitution," &c., &c., &c., Head Master.

ASSISTED BY

Mr. SULIOT, A.M.,	Teacher of French.	Mr. HAMILTON,	Teacher of Nat. Philos. & Chemistry.
Mr. STERN,	„ German.	Mr. PIDGEON,	„ Drawing.
Mr. BUCK,	„ English.	Mr. STEWART.	„ Writing.
Dr. SCOTT,	„ Mathematics.	Mr BURDON.	„ Preparatory Section.

The English, French, German, Latin, and Greek Languages; Geography, History, and Political Economy; Writing and Drawing; Arithmetic and Bookkeeping; the following branches of the Mathematics—Plane and Solid Geometry, Algebra, Trigonometry, Astronomy; Natural Philosophy; Chemistry, and Natural History,

The object aimed at is not merely to afford sound and liberal instruction, but to call into activity and to train the mental powers, so that the pupils may be fully qualified, either for entering on University studies, or for devoting themselves at once to commercial life.

TERMS.

The Fees are from £6 6s. to £12 12s. per Annum, according to the position of the pupils, and are payable in advance at the following dates, and in the following sums:—

	1st April.	1st August.	1st October.	1st January.
1st and 2nd Classes	£3 12 9	£3 12 9	£2 11 9	£3 12 9
3rd and 4th „	3 2 9	3 2 9	1 19 9	3 2 9
5th and 6th „	2 11 2	2 11 2	1 12 6	2 11 2
Preparatory Section	1 19 4	1 6 0	1 19 4	1 19 4

An extra charge of 4s. 6d. per Quarter is made for the Books, Slates, &c., used in School, which are supplied by the Institution. Drawing Books, Paper, Pencils, Chemicals, &c., must be paid for in addition, according to the consumption.

Every Pupil must either be a Member, or the Son or Brother of a Member, of the Institution. The Annual Subscription of a Member is 21s.

An Exhibition to London University, value £200, is open to Competition at next Midsummer Examination.

Several of the Masters receive Pupils as Boarders.

3. GIRLS' SCHOOL, BLACKBURNE HOUSE.

Miss ELLISON, *Matron and Head Governess.*

English Department.—Misses JONES & GARDNER.	*Vocal Music.*—Mr. MOLINEUX.
Arithmetic.—Miss J. NICHOLSON.	*Dancing.*—Mr. J. R. PALMER.
Writing.—Miss NICHOLSON.	*Calisthenic Exercises.*—Mr. T. B. WEDGWOOD.
Needlework.—Misses GREAVES and DAWSON.	*French.*—Mr. T. E. SULIOT, M.A.
Drawing.—Mrs. PEDDER.	*Natural Philosophy & Chemistry.*—Mr. HAMILTON.

This School is designed to afford a sound, comprehensive, and practical education, at a moderate charge. The course of instruction embraces English Reading and Spelling, Grammar, Geography, History, the Derivation of Words, &c., Writing, Arithmetic, Drawing, Needlework, Natural Philosophy and Chemistry, French, Dancing, and Vocal Music.

TERMS.

The Fees are £5 per Annum to the Daughters of Members, payable in advance at the following dates, and in the following sums:—

1st April.	1st August.	1st October.	1st January.
£1 7 4	£1 18 6	£1 7 4	£1 7 4

Other Pupils pay 10s. per Annum additional.

These charges include the use of Books, Slates, Writing and Drawing Books, Pencils, &c., all of which are supplied by the Institution. There is an extra charge for French, Dancing, and Calisthenic Exercises. For the use of Books in the Library of Circulation attached to the School, each Pupil pays 6d. per Quarter.

Some of the Teachers receive Pupils as Boarders.

4. INFANT SCHOOL,

(ATTACHED TO THE GIRLS' SCHOOL.)

Teacher.—Miss LATEY.	*Assistant.*—Miss HAMPSON.

This School is designed for the education of Children of both sexes, under six years of age, and is meant to prepare them for entering the regular Day Schools. The instruction given consists of Easy Lessons in Reading and Spelling, Writing, Drawing, &c., combined with amusing occupations. The greatest attention is paid to the training of the Children to habits of kindness, truthfulness, &c.

TERMS.

The Fees are £2 2s. per Annum to the Children of Members, payable in advance at the following dates, and in the following sums:—

1st April.	1st August.	1st October.	1st January.
11s. 8d.	7s. 0d.	11s. 8d.	11s. 8d.

Other Pupils pay 6s. per Annum additional.

The Annual Examination takes place in all the Day Schools during the second week of June.

The Holidays are six weeks at Midsummer, commencing about the middle of June; two weeks at Christmas, commencing about 23rd December, and four days at Easter.

Persons inclined to forward the objects of the Institution, by distributing this Prospectus in Work Shops, &c. will be supplied with copies on application at the Institution.

THE

DOMESTIC GYMNASIUM, REGISTERED,

OR,

PORTABLE GYMNASTIC APPARATUS,

INVENTED BY

MONSIEUR LOUIS HUGUENIN,

Teacher of Gymnastics in Liverpool; Originator and formerly Proprietor of various Gymnasia, in London, Bristol, Dublin, &c. &c.

SOLD AT HIS

GYMNASIUM, LIVERPOOL;

WITH

ANATOMICAL AND MEDICAL OBSERVATIONS,

BY

CHARLES EDWARD HERBERT ORPEN, M.D., M.R.I.A.

———

UNDER THE PATRONAGE OF

THE COUNTESS AND EARL OF SEFTON.

═══════════════════════════

The principal Exercises for which this Apparatus supplies means may, for distinction sake, be named as follows; and I prefer giving them self-explanatory *English names*, which the public can understand at once, to inventing even more euphonious compound *Greek* or *Latin* terms, which would require long explanations. I write, also, for everybody, not merely for the learned in my own profession.

1st.—The UNDER-SAWYER EXERCISE, calling into play the same aggregate set of muscles as are used by the *under Sawyer*, in a pit, if not assisted by the *upper* or *top Sawyer* in dragging down the saw to cut the beam; and this may be practised with one or both arms.

2d.—The PULL-ROWING EXERCISE, in which the machine affords an exercise almost exactly similar to that of *rowing a boat*, while we are sitting on a bench, or thwart, as is the common custom in these countries, and pulling the handle of the oar towards us, against the resistance of the water at its blade. This may be done with one or both hands.

3d.—The CHEST-EXPANDING EXERCISE, for opening the Chest, or Breast, and strengthening the Muscles in front of the Thorax, or Chest, and of the Shoulders, of one or both sides.

4th.—The GRASP-WINDLASS, or ROLLER-WINDLASS EXERCISE, for strengthening the muscles of the Thumbs, Fingers, Hands, Wrist, and Forearms, in six different ways, the hands either being both at once, or alternately, prone and supine.

5th.—The HANDLES, instead of Parallel Bars, exercise all the extensor muscles of the arms, and very strongly the pectoral muscles ; and, by swinging the legs backwards and forwards, it exercises both extensors and flexors of the body and legs.

6th.—The HORIZONTAL BAR brings into action all the flexor muscles of the arms, scapula, and muscles under the arms, abdomen, &c. These two last constitute almost all the apparatus used in Germany to teach Gymnastics. The justly celebrated Professor Liebig, when he saw MONSIEUR HUGUENIN'S Portable Gymnasium, said, " It is the most ingenious and scientific invention a human being could conceive; and to find out the way of exercising all the muscles of the body must have been the work of many many years' practice, observation, and deep study."

7th.—The TOP-SAWYER EXERCISE, for strengthening the same muscles of the Back, and of one or both Arms, as are used by the *upper Sawyer*, over the beam, if not helped by the *under Sawyer*, in the pit, to raise the saw.

8th.—The ARCHERY EXERCISE, giving power to the same muscles that are used in pulling the string of a strong bow, with either hand.

9th.—The ACTION and RE-ACTION, or ROPE-PULLING EXERCISE, affording nearly the same exertion to the muscles as in pulling an endless rope with one or both hands.

10th.—The TRACTION and RE-TRACTION, or HORSE-RESISTING EXERCISE, calling into play the same entire set of muscles of one or both arms and sides of the body as would be used in pulling against a horse, who was starting or backing from us, while we were standing on the ground and holding him by the head, by a bridle, rope, lasso, or reins.

11th.—The PUSH-ROWING EXERCISE, which cultivates the same muscles as are used in rowing a boat in the Mediterranean, where the rower stands and pushes at the middle of the oar forward and from him, with either one or both hands.

12th.—The SCULLING EXERCISES, giving play to the same set of muscles are as used in *sculling a boat*, with one oar at the stern ; and this with two hands, or only one.

13th.—The SEMI-ROTARY EXERCISE of the sides and back of the Chest, Abdomen, and Loins ; especially for strengthening the *obliquely* acting muscles of each side of the Chest and Abdomen, by which the body is turned half or quarter round, as in the *wrestling, pitching a stone, throwing a quoit, &c.*

There are, perhaps, a hundred other varied exercises to which this excellent apparatus may be made subservient, but it is needless to specify them all in detail, or to give them names. Each person will invent some for himself, and MONS. HUGUENIN will explain the chief of those that I have mentioned, and many others, to any one who wishes to purchase one of his Machines, which occupies a small space in a room, is rather ornamental than otherwise, is a great amusement to children, and will often keep them employed and out of mischief, to the great relief of parents, and to their own benefit, on dull, wet, and idle days.

The cost is only a few pounds, and varies, of course, according to the size, materials, and complexity of the Apparatus, and the number of exercises for which it is calculated.

GYMNASTICS,

AND THE

DOMESTIC GYMNASIUM.

HAVING been very much impressed with the importance of GYM-NASTIC EXERCISES, as an indispensable branch of the Physical Education of all children, from witnessing their good effects both at Schools and at regular Gynasiums, while travelling on the Continent many years ago, I was highly gratified, when I found that MONSIEUR LOUIS HUGUENIN had fixed his residence in Dublin, and begun a systematic Gymnastic School there, shortly after my own settlement in that city, as a practitioner of Medicine aud Surgery; and I believe that I was, consequently, the first professional man in that metropolis who gave him a certificate of their value, which I did in the strongest terms. Similar certificates were subsequently given to him by almost all the Surgeons and Physicians, of the greatest eminence, in Dublin, and in various other cities of Ireland and England; and he established similar Gymnasia in several other cities and towns, which were afterwards either conducted by his pupils, or sold to others.

Every year's experience since, of their beneficial effects upon patients, or acquaintances of my own, or of other medical men, has only served to convince me still more of their importance; and I know this to be the opinion of every Physician and Surgeon with whom I have conversed.

I have also made all my children practice Gymnastic Exercises from an early age, and the results have been most satisfactory and encouraging; not only by manifest benefit to their health and increase of strength, but also by improvement of form and by greater presence of mind in danger, from increased self-confidence and an internal consciousness of power.

It has been objected by some persons to the use of Gymnastics during childhood, adolescence, and youth, that they will tend, by the increased power of the muscles, to stunt the growth, and to prevent the elongation of the bones; deducting, in fact, from *stature* what they give in *broadness of chest* and *bulk of limbs;* but this is altogether as untrue in fact, as it can be predicted to be necessarily false, by physiological laws. I have seven sons, who have all practised Gymnastics regularly since they were little children; those who are already grown up are nearly as tall, or taller, than myself, (five feet ten inches and three-quarters, without shoes;) and also as stout or stronger: and every one of the younger ones gives promise of a similar result.

It has been said, that Gymnastics interfere with the cultivation of the mind, but this is directly contrary to the fact. Of course if any person spent his entire time in exercise and neglected study wholly, the result would be a want of mental culture, as it would be if he spent all his time in mere play, or idleness; but the regular use of Gymnastics has a most decidedly beneficial effect, both upon the activity of the mind, and on its power of continuous study, without injury to the health; and this, for very evident reasons, especially amongst the upper classes of society, one great misfortune of whom is, that, by full diet, insufficient exercise, too little ventilation of their lungs and skin in the open air, too luxurious ease in drawing-rooms and bed-rooms, a great tendency to accumulation of blood in the head becomes habitual at an early age; and the lungs, with all the subsidiary parts of the chest and the muscles of respiration, are also badly developed. Gymnastic Exercises, by turning away the current of blood from the brain and spinal marrow towards the muscles, not only cause these to grow, but relieve the nervous matter of the brain from too great pressure and obstruction by the blood, or by large and distended blood-vessels; while, on the contrary, by the cultivation of the muscles of respiration, and by the expansion of all the bones and parietes of the chest, or thorax, they give greater space for the lungs to expand and play in, and consequently facilitate the transmission of blood through all their vessels. This necessarily increases the purification of the blood by respiration; for the more perfectly *carbon* is removed from the venous, impure, spoiled, and dark blood in the lungs, and the more entirely this is re-changed into bright arterial blood by the absorption of *oxygen*, the purer of course must be the blood, which is driven by the heart to the brain, which is thus triply bene-fitted,—first, by diminished pressure; secondly, by the removal of stupe-fying narcotized blood; and thirdly, by the presence and natural stimulus of pure arterialised blood. The *brain* is undoubtedly not the *mind*, nor the master of the mind, nor even the dominant organ of the mind, as productive of its faculties; but it is the subsidiary organ of the mind, as being a vital *nervo-electric** apparatus, of which the spirit, soul, or mind makes use in its operations; just as the muscles, tendons, and bones are a mechanical apparatus of levers, pulleys, and vital motive powers, of which our mental, or corporal, will makes use in bodily movements; or as the stomach, liver, &c. are true chemical apparatuses which our animal, or organic life, makes use of in secretion, digestion, &c.

I have commonly also practised Gymnastic Exercises myself, with my children, and found them exceedingly beneficial, not only to my muscular strength, but to all the functions connected with respiration, digestion, and transpiration.

They have a most decidedly good effect also in removing *nervousness*, by preventing determination of blood to the head and spinal marrow, by producing perspiration and transpiration, through the skin and lungs, and by turning away the current of blood towards the muscles and limbs; and, in producing thus calmness of internal feelings, removing irritability and

---

* I use the word *nervo-electric* in preference to *electro-magnetic*, as more exactly expressing my meaning; and also because the word *magnetic* is open to objections and cavils, having now two acceptations, viz.. magnetism, as in a few metals, and magnetism, as in the novel sense of mesmerism, or hypnotism.

excitability, and procuring sleep; insomuch that I have no doubt that they have thus, incidentally and secondarily, what we may almost call a moral influence, especially on the young.

Many years ago MONSIEUR HUGUENIN made for me a Gymnastic Apparatus, which I could put up in my back drawing-room, in Dublin, for my children to use on wet days. He has since made very many for others, and I have been so gratified by the remarkable improvements, extensions, and simplifications, which he has gradually introduced, upon his first conceptions, that I have at once willingly acceded to his request, to write a brief explanation of its construction, applications, and chief advantages, with a few Anatomical and Medical Observations subjoined.

MONSIEUR HUGUENIN was held in the highest esteem by the whole Medical and Surgical profession in Dublin, who constantly sent delicate persons, and especially the young, or those who, while growing up, were threatened with any deformity of the spine, or chest, from weakness, to him, in order that he might make them pursue an appropriate system of exercises, adapted to the weaker parts, or muscles; which had frequently the happiest results. Even elderly persons, too, were often cured, or greatly relieved of Dyspeptic and Stomach Complaints; while Affections of the Breathing, and Nervous Headaches, were often also removed. Yet, even still, medical men and the public, and especially mothers, are not sufficiently alive to the value of Gymnastics, as a subsidiary branch of the healing art, in preventing or curing Chronic complaints.

So great has been the care and attention given by MONSIEUR HUGUENIN to his pupils, that from his first settlement in Dublin to the present time, I have never known nor heard of an accident, of any moment, occurring in his Gymnasiums.

And I feel it but justice to MONSIEUR HUGUENIN to say, that he is one of the most assiduous and persevering teachers, that I have ever known; equally remarkable for good temper, cheerfulness, and patience; and though I have been many hundred times present in his Gymnasiums, formerly in Dublin, and of late years in that of Liverpool, I have witnessed the most decisive good effects of these qualities upon his pupils, in my never having seen the least disagreement amongst them, though often contending together in rival exercises of strength and feats of agility.

I have also the highest respect for MONSIEUR HUGUENIN'S personal character, as a gentleman, and a man of an honourable and upright mind.

I shall now proceed to my immediate object. But as the mechanical construction of the DOMESTIC GYMNASIUM will be best understood by an ocular examination of it, at MONSIEUR HUGUENIN'S, it is needless to waste the reader's time, with a minute verbal description of the construction of

THE PORTABLE GYMNASTIC APPARATUS.

This ingenious Apparatus combines the following, amongst other great advantages :

1st.—That it is capable of being erected at a comparatively small expense.

2d.—That it can be placed and used, in any room of ordinary size, in one's dwelling-house.

3d.—That it may, when necessary, be taken to pieces and packed in a box of moderate dimensions, and removed like other furniture; and can, therefore, be sent to any part of the kingdom, or exported.

4th.—That yet I know, as an Anatomist, that by its various contrivances it may be used, so as to cultivate the strength of almost all the chief sets and classes of muscles in the body, whether Flexors or Extensors, Adductors or Abductors, Pronators or Supinators, &c., and this not only of the trunk of the body, (including the neck, chest, or thorax, abdomen and waist, shoulders and back,) and of the chief articulations of the upper and lower limbs, but of many of the smaller joints also, viz., of the wrist, hand and fingers, of the ancle, foot and toes.

5th. —That it will thus enable all persons, especially on wet and chilly days, and particularly those who are much confined by their business to offices or desks, or to any one habitual posture of the body, or to sedentary study or teaching, to exercise, at will, almost all their muscles in one hour, as much as they could by any other contrivance in several hours.

6th.—That thus these varied exercises may be placed within the reach of all classes of society, and will be found invaluable, especially to the higher ranks, and more particularly to growing children and young females; for, though their common and only exercises of walking, skipping, dancing, &c., and a little more those of riding, &c., do exercise, in a tolerably fair degree, the lower limbs, and the lower half of the body, as far up as the waist, yet they afford no adequate exercise for the upper half of the body, including the thorax or chest, the sides and shoulders, the whole back-bone, loins, and arms; which is the chief cause, among young persons, of both sexes, in the upper classes of society, why we so often find the upper half of the body, from the waist upwards, so badly developed; the chest and breast contracted, the back-bone curved, the breast-bone flattened, or sometimes, as it is called, chicken-breasted and projecting; the shoulders so round, and the arms weak. This is especially the case in Females, and particularly among young ladies, who have so much fewer resources of exercises than males have; and it is the main reason why so many of them have narrow and sunken chests, ill-developed breasts, uneven shoulders, and curved spines; all of which are not merely visible external deformities, but really productive internally of much displacement and pressure, and of much illness and discomfort; and also of serious injury to their health and usefulness in many ways; for it is an established fact in Anatomy, and a law in Physiology, that these external malformations are invariably accompanied, either as reciprocal cause or effect, by internal defects in development, especially of the lungs, and of all the organs of respiration, of which they are a sure index.

That Gymnastic Exercises are indispensible to health and to the free motion of the limbs, all persons can easily conceive, since exercise, in some manner or other, is natural to man and to all animals; and the old proverb, that "practice makes perfect," is well illustrated by the fact, that the repetition of any motion will render that motion not only more easily performed, but capable also of being repeated for a long time with less fatigue.

Every body has heard of, and many thousands in this country have witnessed the various dances of the North American Indians, especially those exhibited by Mr. Catlin, namely, their War Dance, Buffalo Dance, Dog Dance, &c.; but few persons, perhaps, have considered the reason for which they practice these, or the benefits, which, in their savage state of life, they derive from them. What, then, is the real and unsuspected motive and effect of such exercises? Certainly not mere amusement, for the time. The Indian is naturally of a melancholic disposition, or, to speak more correctly, of a reflecting meditative cast of mind. These exercises are always practised by them for a few days, before entering on any warlike expedition, or indeed on any undertaking, such as a great hunting excursion. They consist chiefly in a quick kind of step, with greater motion of the lower limbs than in walking, the feet are raised high and the body lifted up, by elastic springs of the feet and legs, the hatchet or tomahawk is brandished aloft, or the spear poised, and the body is energetically swayed in all directions: the whole is a most fatiguing exercise, and yet it is practised for several days prior to the laborious undertaking that they have in view. Without physiological reasoning upon it, the Indians have found this practically the most effectual mode of strengthening their bodies, of making their joints supple, and of training themselves for either inflicting or avoiding wounds, attacking or escaping. The oiling or smearing of the body too, used by some, and the excitement which is a concomitant of these violent exercises, help them in this preparation; and by the song or recitative, which accompanies their movements and regulates them, the whole becomes not a mere dull practice, but a spirit-stirring exercise, in which, of course, emulation also plays no little part.

To confirm these by an example and an experiment, that any one can make, whose occupations oblige him to walk a good deal, whereby that exercise has become an acquired habit and a kind of second nature to the muscles used; such a person, if he remains casually quiet for a whole day, or is long sitting, as for example during a holiday, or when any particular business requires it, will find his legs, feet, knees, hips, and back often become quite *weary with rest* and even feel them aching; let him under these circumstances begin to practice any exercises, like these Indian dances, and if he carries them on energetically and long enough, say immoderately for half an hour, he will find their effect equivalent to a very long promenade; the weariness, aching and lassitude will disappear, he will breathe afterwards more freely, and be able to sit down again to his sedentary work for the rest of the day with more vigour. Gymnastic Exercises and Machines can evidently effect this relief much sooner and more completely.

In speaking of the benefits of Gymnastics in the Physical Education of Females, I should not omit to allude to the pernicious effects of stays. Eastern ladies, and indeed all Asiatic females, never wear them; and hence it is that they have such beautifully formed busts, expanded chests, pyramidal breasts, and uniform shoulders. I have often, in dissecting, found the shape of the lungs, and still more that of the liver completely altered, by the habitual use of stays during growth; and as all the organs contained in the chest, or near the stomach, are amongst those most essential to life, as being those of digestion, nutrition, respiration, and calorification, an injury to their size, free play, and perfect functions must above all other things interfere with health. Man and all similar animals, vertebral, or mammal, have their bones internal and their flesh outside them; lobsters and such animals have their flesh internal and their bones external; but a tight-laced fine lady is of neither class, for, what with spring-supplied stays or bodices, she has her muscles crushed between internal bones and external whalebone or steel; and what is worse than all, the lungs, heart, liver, and stomach are compressed and crushed into a small space by this whole artificial apparatus. Certainly of late years our neighbours, the

French, have much improved the material, tissue, cutting out, fitting, and manufacture of stays, or rather bodices; but even the best of these pieces of female armour prevent the lateral and forward expansion of the chest, (by the elevation or protusion of the anterior ends of the ribs and the turning out of their lower edges, by means of the action of the double intercostal muscles,) and they compel almost the whole act of breathing to be performed by the diaphragm, a large flat thin muscle between the lungs and stomach. This not only compresses needlessly the stomach and liver, but allows the lungs to expand only from above downwards, scarcely at all from side to side, and still less from back to front, as the stays compress the ribs upon each other and the breast bone towards the back. Hence the shape of the lungs becomes changed and unnatural, many of the muscles of the ribs, sides, chest, and back cease their growth, or even become smaller; and are eventually partially atrophied, or at least not fully developed. The long life and health of all persons, especially the fitness of women to be good nurses, depend very much on the size of the lungs and chest, &c., and the developement of all these parts is impeded by stays. By substituting also the support of external steel or whalebone, for the internal strength of bones and ligaments, and the gradual growth of muscles, to keep all these in their proper places, young women often incur such weakness of the bones, ligaments, and muscles of the spine, as ends in those lateral curvatures, which deform the shape of so many young ladies. All parts of the body waste and get weaker by inaction; they grow and are kept in health by appropriate exercise and use, suitable to their functions. There is also another most injurious invention, advertised in almost every periodical, and called, I believe, a Back Stretcher, or Chest Expander, which is after all only a kind of stays made in leather, and employed chiefly for boys, who however will inevitably grow every day more crooked and their backs weaker during its use. It is in some respects worse than stays, because by the help of the straps and buckles it can be so tightened as to weigh down the shoulders, and by its continual downward pressure it tends to prevent the vertical growth of the vertebræ, while at the same time it will cause the neck to bend forward, as a natural consequence of the pulling backwards and downwards of the shoulders. It might well be called a back-crusher.

I may here observe, that persons who carry weights on their heads, as fish-women in the street, are remarkable for holding themselves erect and straight, and never have a stoop or a curved spine. One of the most effectual means of removing stooping, and even of checking incipient *lateral* curvature of the spine, is by making the patient carry weights on the head, gradually augmented; this compels all the muscles, by which perpendicularity is produced and preserved, to exert themselves, and by this exertion they grow; and as the body cannot be allowed either to bend forward or to either side, the muscles gradually pull all the bones and ligaments into their proper position, and keep them, as well as themselves, in due posture. In fact, lateral curvature is caused by disproportioned strength, or exertion of different lateral sets of muscles, and by relaxation of ligaments, and can only be cured by producing a contrary state, by exercise and a well-balanced perpendicularity of spine; never by either artificial machines, nor by mere rest. The peasantry in those parts of the country where it is the custom to carry burdens on the head, are remarkable for their erect stature and ease of motion. This is well seen about Aveyron, in France.

I may mention here a curious illustration I once had of the beneficial effects of muscular action locally, in a kind of partial gymnastics, produced by accidental disease. One of my own sons had a narrow chest, when a baby, and his breast-bone projected in the manner that is called chicken-breasted. He got hooping-cough when very young, and had it severely, though not dangerously, for several months; the cough, of course, threw all the muscles of respiration, and especially those of expiration, into violent exercise; and by the time that he was well of the hooping-cough, his breast-bone had sunk, by having been dragged into its proper place, and was quite flat; his ribs had spread out laterally, and his chest was broad and well formed, and it has remained so ever since. I have no doubt that the lungs increased in size at the same time and from the same cause, and have continued, with all the rest of the chest, to grow properly.

ANATOMICAL, PHYSIOLOGICAL, AND MEDICAL OBSERVATIONS.

Having thus explained, in a popular and intelligible manner, the chief applications of the Apparatus, my readers will be better able to understand the few Anatomical and other observations, that I shall now make on each particular exercise, in order to give a general idea of the separate parts of the body, whose muscles are exercised, and of course strengthened, by each; for it is a law of every part of our body, that exercise, with perhaps a little degree of moderate fatigue, followed by adequate rest, is an essential element in enabling nutrition to cause growth and strength, as well as in increasing the flexibility, mobility and activity, of each part. And I believe that the same law precisely is universally applicable to our intellectual faculties and moral powers, namely, that attentive exertion, with voluntary and repeated exercise, carried just to the borders of commencing exhaustion, are indispensable to the attainment, retention, ready use and reproduction of knowledge, in subjection to our will, and that we never can advance, or grow, or become strong, in either intellect, moral power, or spiritual virtue, except by the appropriate exercise of our rational powers, moral feelings, and spiritual faculties, on their appropriate objects, or duties, and in their specific ways.

The body never becomes stronger except by nutrition, exercise, and growth; neither can the mind ever improve, except by observation, reflection, study, and the use of our mental faculties, at will; nor, as to moral feelings, does any one ever become more kind, benevolent, or forgiving, by merely thinking of the duty, but exclusively by exercising it on appropriate objects; and as to spiritual, or, what have sometimes been called, supernatural faculties, no man ever did grow in grace, faith, hope, or love, to God or man, except by exercising the faculty and the duty, namely, by obeying, believing, hoping, trusting, confiding and loving. It is of the utmost importance in medicine, education, government and religion, to be convinced of this universal law of the complex nature of man. And I believe that Gymnastics, by helping to fix in our minds, as to our physical nature and the mechanical parts of our body, the conviction of the fact, that all exertion must be progressive, that strength can only be increased by suitable exercise, and that all successful efforts and exertions depend upon the previous gradual cultivation of power in our muscles, contribute to fix also in our minds the truth, that similar laws apply to the intellectual and moral nature of our compound being. Looking at others practising Gymhastics will never strengthen us, though it may help to shew us how best to proceed, in order to cultivate and retain strength; and precisely so it is with intellect, ethics, morals, habits, and piety; each man must exert himself for his self-education, in all these relations, according to the metaphysical and moral laws of our nature, established by God himself at its creation, who formed all things in harmony, who makes every thing active, who wishes for our progress, and abhors sloth, inactivity, retrogression, tergiversation, and back sliding.

In explaining briefly the chief allied sets of muscles, that are used concomitantly in each exercise, it is, of course, necessary, as I am writing not for medical men alone, but for the general public, that I should avoid entering too minutely into an analysis of all the movements of the body, or using any terms, that would be understood only by Anatomists. I shall, therefore, confine myself merely to such general remarks, as may be intelligible to all readers, premising only a very few words of necessary preliminary explanations.

Flexor Muscles, or Flexors, mean those that bend any joint of the limbs, head, neck, or trunk; as, for example, into the easy bent posture, that our limbs assume, when we are sleeping on our side in bed, which is one of the greatest ease and rest. The Flexor Muscles are generally the strongest in the body.

Extensor Muscles, or Extensors, include all those that do the exact contrary of the Flexors; that is, which bring the joints, limbs, and trunk into a straight position, or that in which they were before the Flexors bent them; they, therefore, straighten the limbs and trunk. The Extensors are in general not nearly so strong as the Flexors, because we evidently require to do more, make more exertion, lift greater weights, &c. by bending than extending our joints and limbs. The reason, why we yawn and stretch ourselves when we awake, is to call the Extensors again into activity, and so to enable them to stretch the Flexors, which had been rather contracted during sleep.

Adductor Muscles, or Adductors, mean all those that draw the opposite limbs together, or any lateral part of the body, towards an imaginary middle line, or plane, that would divide the body, equally, into two side halves, viz., right and left: as, for example, when we draw our knees together, to catch anything thrown, or dropped, into our lap; or when we press our arms against our sides, to carry some weight between them.

Abductor Muscles, or Abductors, mean and do exactly the reverse; thus they separate the opposite limbs from each other, or move any lateral part of the body away from the imaginary mesial plane, or middle plane, or line, that partitions the whole body into two lateral halves, right and left; as, for example, when we separate our knees while sitting or our feet widely when standing. The Abductor Muscles are not nearly as strong as the Adductors, for we much more frequently require to approximate our two legs, or our arms to our sides, than to separate them with any force: the former, therefore, require less strength naturally, and acquire less by habitual use.

Pronator Muscles, or Pronators, mean those that perform such a motion of the fore-arms, as turns the palms of our hands downwards, as in laying our hands on the table, with the backs uppermost, or as in screw-driving.

Supinator Muscles, or Supinators, do the exact reverse, and, therefore, turn the palms upwards, which was the position used by the ancient

Heathens in praying, viz., with supine hands, to what they ignorantly called the heavenly deities, in contradistinction to the infernal deities, in praying to whom they used the former posture, namely, prone palms. The Supinators are never as strong as the Pronators. And in confirmation of this, I may remark, that it is a curious fact, that right-hand screws are what are almost universally made to be used, and left-hand screws very rarely, for these very obvious reasons,—first, that almost all men use the right hand in preference to the left; and, secondly, that the muscles used in pronation, that is, semirotation forwards and inwards, are much more powerful, and, therefore, more easily used with effect, than those that produce supination, that is, semirotation backwards and outwards.

Rotator Muscles, or Rotators, are those which rotate or turn any bone, joint, limb, or part of the body partially round, generally only a quarter, never more than half, (unless where there is excessive looseness and mobility of the joints, as in tumblers and stage-dancers,) as in turning our toes out straight, while our heels are touching, as in one of the positions in learning to dance, or in making the spread-eagle in skating. The muscles, that rotate the bones or limbs forwards and inwards, are stronger, in general, than those that rotate them outwards and backwards, because the former movements are more required aud more used.

Oblique muscles are those that move any part of the body in an oblique or sloping manner, half way between bending forwards or to one side, and rotating, as in bending and turning half round, to bow to a person at one side of us, or behind us.

There are a variety of other classes of Muscles, with a vast diversity of names, but it would be almost impossible to explain them to general readers, without tedious minuteness and numerous diagrams, and would also only lead to confusion; and in the application of even the above very extensive classes of names, Anatomists have often in fact not been as precise as they should have been in attending to the exact action of each Muscle *by itself*, but have often misapplied the names, or given them to express rather a *combined* action with other Muscles, than their own single and separate action. This, however, cannot now be remedied either by myself or my readers; let us, therefore, pass on with one remark, that no one set of Muscles ever acts alone, for in order to have a fixed point, towards which any set of Muscles may act, and pull any other part, it is necessary that some other set of Muscles should act to fix that point, and so, in fact, the necessity for the assisting action of the Muscles extends sometimes through successive sets of Muscles, to the most remote parts of the body; and in this way the strong action of one set of Muscles may necessitate more or less of Muscular action all over the body, in order to enable them to act with energy towards their fixed points.

It is necessary also to explain, that the different sets of Muscles are antagonist to each other, thus the Flexors and Extensors, the Adductors and Abductors, the Pronators and Supinators, the Rotators outwards, and the Rotators inwards, &c., &c., are reciprocally antagonistic; and the truth is, that antagonist muscles always act together, the one set strongly to produce the desired motion, the opposite set weakly, in order to keep the joints tight, to regulate the movement and prevent jerks. Hence it is, that if one set of Muscles be cut across, the will loses its power over their antagonists. This is a point that is very generally unknown or overlooked.

A few brief observations upon the chief actions of Muscles in each exercise, will now suffice for all useful purposes; actual inspection and practice, with explanations of the Machine, on the spot, by MONS. HUGUENIN, must accomplish the rest.

1st.—In the PULL-ROWING EXERCISE, as the under surface of the Toes and the Soles of the Feet are fixed against the sloping Foot-board, while one is sitting on the stool and pulling, by means of closed hands, flexing forearms, and extending upper-arms, (humeri,) the handle, to which the rope, passing through three successive pulleys, and having a weight suspended at the other end, is attached, while at the same time we draw our heads and trunk backwards, so as to make our whole Body, Head, Neck, Trunk, and lower Limbs, nearly in one straight line, it is evident that our Toes and Feet are the chief fixed points; just as all sailors, sitting on the thwarts, or benches, of a boat, have their Feet pressed against one of the ribs of the boat, one of the stretchers, or another bench, and that we, like them, exert either simultaneously or in succession, the following Muscles, namely, the Flexors of the joints of the Toes, and of the Soles of the Feet, the Extensors of the Ancle Joints and whole Foot. And several muscles that are more commonly used as Flexors of the Knee-joints upon the Thighs, when fixed, and Extensors of the Hip-joints upon the Trunk, when fixed, are now used together as Extensors of the Trunk on the Hips, because the lower Limbs are more fixed. The Extensors of the Back, and the Flexors of the Neck, are all used at the same time. And as to the upper Limbs, or Arms, the Flexors of the Joints of the Fingers and Palms of the Hands, Wrists, and Elbows, are used either in Grasping or Pulling, and the Extensors of the upper Arms, with many large and small muscles, that move the Shoulder Blades and Collar Bones are called into action, either to move them slightly backwards, especially the lower angles of the Shoulder Blade, or else to make them fixed points, towards which the whole Arms can be drawn.

There are many minor movements of joints, and contractions, or relaxations of muscles, involved in this exercise, which it would be tedious to particularize; but, from this brief review, it is evident, that a vast variety of muscles, from the Toes to the Head, are called into exertion by this one Exercise alone. Restoring all the Limbs and Jointsto their former posture will also, of course, call into action all the Muscles, that are Antagonists to those that I have mentioned, but with less effect and less force. And the fact, that such a great number of Muscles is called into action, during the successive movements of this well-contrived exercise, proves it to be one of the very best, and strongest efforts, that we can make, particularly when the body is nearly extended.

It is evident, however, that as the weights would pull back the Handle, without any effort on our part, this Exercise does not call into full play those Muscles, that are used in Rowing, to push the Oar Handle forward again into its first place, nor those used in feathering the blade of the Oar, as it is called, during the forward movement of its handle, and backward movement of the blade, through the air. The former of these movements will however be found in the next exercise, namely:

2d.—The PUSH-ROWING EXERCISE. In this the person exercising stands with his back to the front of the Machine, (not his face, as in the previous sitting posture,) with his feet on the ground, his right and left foot alternately advanced a little farther from it, than the other, as in the antique statues of the Athletes or Boxer, and of the Discobolos, or Quoit Player, and catching one of the leather-covered handles in each hand, he pushes them alternately forward to the full length of his Arms, so as to raise the appended weight behind, and then he lets the weights draw his arms back to their former position, by their own weight gradually, not ever by a jerk, or by a sudden relaxation of the muscles. A jerk is always to be avoided in Gymnastics, for if used to contract the muscles, it may sometimes overstrain them and the joints, or if used in a sudden relaxation of the muscles, it in no degree strengthens them, and might cause the weight suspended, whatever it is, to strain the muscles at any moment, or to sprain the joints at the close. Every weight should be lifted gradually, and let down in the same way; and every exertion of muscles should be graduated, by which means the strength is measured, exerted, and increased, without danger, and their relaxation should be gradual also, by which means their strength, with that of their antagonist muscles, is still further developed, without the risk of any sudden violence, jerk, or twist.

This exercise may be used with both arms, or with one, or with each alternately, and, in all these varieties, it is evidently very like the exercise of rowing, as practised in the Mediterranean, (or in this country, in rowing with sweeps, which are very long and heavy oars,) when the rower stands up in the boat, or on the deck, and pushes the handle of the oar, or sweep, from him and forwards, by which motion of course the blade is made to move backwards, because his face is turned towards the head or prow of the boat, that is, towards the place whither he is rowing, which is a kind of go-a-head method, and just the contrary of our common English way of rowing, while sitting, in which the rower has his back to the prow of the boat, and of course to his destined harbour, while his face regards and looks back upon the course that he has already traversed, as if in retrospection.

In this exercise the feet are fixed on the ground, the head leaning forward, and the arms and hands are gradually pushed forwards to their full length, to raise the weight behind, and are then allowed to be drawn upwards and backwards gradually by the sinking of the weight. It is evident, therefore, that though some muscles, used in the former exercise, are also exerted in this, yet there are others of a quite different class also called into play. The Flexors of the toes and soles of the feet are used. The Flexors of the feet on the ancles and legs, are used as Flexors of the legs on the ancles and feet, because the feet are fixed points. The Extensors of the legs and knee-joints upon the thighs are used for the same reason, as Extensors of the thighs and knee-joints upon the legs. The Flexors of the thighs and hip-joints upon the trunk are used as Flexors of the trunk and hip-joints upon the thighs. The Anterior Flexors of the trunk also are used to bend it; and, as to the arms, the Extensors of the hands, fore-arms, and arms, are used along with various muscles of the neck, that either move or fix the collar-bones and the shoulder-blades, and the various muscles of the collar-bones and the shoulder-blades that move the arms forwards, and many others of the neck, chest, and back, that either move forward, or fix, the arm-bones, collar-bones, and shoulder-blades.

3d.—In the SCULLING EXERCISE, we stand before the Machine, and, taking one of the handles in each hand, we pull and push at the same time the handle that is in the right-hand towards the left, and then, alternately, the handle that is in the left-hand towards the right; semi-rotating our body at each movement, and at the same time inclining it, first to one side and then to the other, somewhat as is done in sculling a boat with both hands. This exertion evidently calls into action the oblique and rotary muscles of the trunk upon the hips, and also all those muscles, abductors, and others, which help to move the arms towards the side, and push the hands across the chest, and of course the antagonists of all these are exercised in recovering the first position. All the Flexors and Extensors, also, of the thighs, legs, and feet, and of the trunk, and also of the arms, are more or less called into action, to afford fixed points.

4th.—The fourth Exercise, in which both handles are held *at once* by both hands, calls into action very nearly the same sets of muscles as the last, so that I may pass it over. It is more laborious than the former.

5th.—In the TOP-SAWYER EXERCISE, the chief muscles employed are the Extensors of the trunk, placed upon the back, to straighten it in rising, and to afford fixed points for the muscles of the arms to act towards; the Abductors of the arms, the Flexors of the fore-arms and of the hands and fingers are used, while at the same time, of course, almost all the muscles of the thighs, legs, and feet must act, partly to assist in raising the weight, and partly to produce fixed points. All the muscles also, that move the lower angles of the shoulder-blades forward, are very much exercised.

6th.—In the UNDER-SAWYER EXERCISE, the Flexors of the trunk, placed in front of it and of the thighs, act to depress the shoulders, bend the body forward and give fixed points for the arms to be drawn towards; and on the arms the chief muscles acting are the Abductors of the arms, the Flexors of the fore-arms, wrists, hands, and fingers; the muscles of the legs do little, except to keep them steady and give fixed points; but many muscles of the shoulder-blades act, especially those that carry their inferior angles nearer to the spine, or back-bone, which is just contrary to that action of the antagonist muscles, in the Top-sawyer Exercise, which carries the same inferior angles of the shoulder-blades forward, towards the chest and away from the back-bone. The flat shoulder-blades have in both these exercises a kind of semirotary movement, on their own axis, over the flat surfaces of the ribs, and of the intercostal muscles between them.

7th.—In the CHEST-EXPANDING EXERCISE the person stands with his back against the cushion, and catches one of the two handles in each hand, and pushes both his arms forward, at the same time, to their full length; and then, separating his hands and arms gradually from each other, upwards, until at full length, he lets them be dragged downwards, backwards, and to each side, by the weights, until his hands and arms are beyond his sides, and then, lastly, he brings his hands to his sides by bending his arms. In the first part of this exercise, the chief muscles used are the Extensors of the hands, wrists, fore-arms, and elbows; in the second part, the Flexors that are antagonist to these, but more particularly the two greater and lesser Pectoral muscles, which being on the front and sides of the chest, or thorax, are partly Abductors of the shoulder-blades and arm-bones, (humeri,) and the larger Pectorals are also Flexors and Rotators, inwards, of the latter bones.

8th.—In the ARCHERY EXERCISE each hand is placed, alternately, on the cushion, to make a fixed point, like holding a bow, and with the other hand, alternately, the handle next it is pulled back as far as the side, or ear, or beyond it, like pulling the string of a bow, and then allowed to be dragged back into its first position by the weight, gradually. It is evident, as to the arms, in this exercise, that while the Flexors are used at one side, the Extensors must be used at the other, and *vice versa.*

In this exercise the whole mass of the muscles attached to the collar-bones, shoulder-blades and arm-bones, (humeri,) act together, more or less, as well as several of those of the back, causing a twisting or semi-rotation of the upper half of the trunk; and, at the same time, the Extensors of the arm which rests against the Machine, and is, in fact, the fixed point of resistance, are called into requisition. I may here make one general remark on all the various exercises, namely, that if any one of them was practised singly, or too much, it would give too great a preponderance of strength, bulk and mobility, to the particular set of muscles, that it called too often into play and activity; but, when all the various exercises are practised in succession, and equally, this can never be the case: for example, this Archery Exercise, if practised alone, would probably give too great roundness to the back and shoulders, but, conjointly with other exercises, which call the Pectorals into exercise, it will produce firmness and due expansion both of the front and back of the shoulders and chest.

9th and 10th.—In these two exercises, namely, ACTION and RE-ACTION, TRACTION and RE-TRACTION, the muscles exercised are nearly the same; and, as in both the feet are the fixed points, a vast variety of muscles all up from the feet to the hands, must be exerted and strengthened. It would take up too much room to detail them all, as I have done above as to other exercises.

11th.—As this GRASP-WINDLASS EXERCISE consists in rolling up the hanging weight, by twisting round the Roller-Windlass, merely by the grasp of both hands, it is evident that it must chiefly, according as either hand is prone or supine, call into play the Flexors or Extensors of the wrists, and the Flexors of the palms and fingers, with some muscles of the fore-arms, arms, (humeri,) collar-bones, and shoulder-blades.

11th and 12th.—As these exercises consist in lifting weights on the palms, or on the backs of the hands, or of the fingers, stretched out straight, it is obvious that they will cultivate the muscular powers, that bend or extend these parts, according as they are turned up or down: they are of less moment than some others.

13th.—The WINCH-WINDLASS EXERCISE calls into action, alternately, the Flexors and Extensors, Adductors and Abductors, of the fore-arms and arms, with many muscles of the shoulder-joints and shoulder-blades. This exercise, from the shifting movements of the arms and body, in consequence of the changing position of the handle of the winch, is a very excellent one for persons who are not very strong, as it calls into play a great variety of muscles in succession. The winch can be taken off the Machine, when not wanted. This exercise should be practised sometimes with both hands, sometimes with only one, and alternately: and also at both sides of the Machine equally.

14th and 15th.—The TREADLE and STIRRUP EXERCISES cultivate chiefly the Flexors of the toes and soles of the feet, the Extensors of the ancles, the Flexors of the knee-joints, and the Extensors of the hip-joints.

On a review of all the exercises it will be evident, that a large majority of them call into activity a great many muscles, especially of the upper limbs and upper half of the body, for which, otherwise, young persons in the higher ranks of society have very little opportunity of exercise. A greater degree of minuteness of explanation, and, above all, diagrams of the movements, would prove this still more, but it would lead me into such detail as would weary my readers, and would double the cost of this brochure, and thus prevent its serving, as much as I wish, the cause of Gymnastics in the hands of MONSIEUR HUGUENIN.

CHARLES EDWARD HERBERT ORPEN, M.D., M.R.I.A.,

Fellow and Member of the Royal Colleges of Surgeons
of Ireland and of England.

14th June, 1845,
34, Hamilton-square, West,
Woodside, Birkenhead, Cheshire.

TREATISE

ON

PHYSICAL EDUCATION.

"Mens sana in corpore sano."—Juv.

CHAPTER I.

A sound mind in a strong and healthy body has been for
ages the grand object of education. How is it, then, that
we commonly forget the improvement of the body, though
we are fully convinced that neither wealth nor titles, neither
learning nor worth, can protect the feeble, the unhealthy,
and the infirm, from the lamentable effects of their condition? Should you have nothing to bequeath your child—
should you bestow on his mind but a narrow education,
still he will bless you, if you form his body to health,
strength, and activity, whether he earns his simple meal,
sweetened by labour, at the plough or the anvil, with the
adze or with the hatchet. On the contrary, while you
cultivate his understanding to the highest pitch, if you neglect the health and strength of his body, could you leave
him the treasure of Orœsus, the debilitated, suffering
wretched, helpless creature would detest the education he
had received, amid all the splendour of reputation, the glare

of honours, and even the incense of a throne. Learning and refinement are to health and bodily perfection, what luxuries are to necessaries. Is not then our education depraved, when it aims at luxury, and neglects our greatest and most essential wants? This thought is the foundation of this Treatise; may it not only be laid to heart, but have a practical effect on education in general! People of rank regard nothing but gracefulness of demeanour.* No sooner has the boy entered his sixth year, than the dancing-master appears, to teach him his positions, &c. &c. But there is a great difference between learning to dance, and forming the body; between elegance of carriage, and muscular strength; between the timid spirit of the young beau, and the manly mind of the rising youth. I love dancing, yet, I am compelled to avow, that this pedantic measurement of steps on a smooth floor, frequently associated with soft, melting passions, contributes little or nothing, as a bodily exercise, to the attainment of a nobler end—to the attainment of that which we would call, in a single word, *manhood*; and is frequently rendered extremely prejudicial to the health of both body and mind, by concomitant circumstances. May it ever be used with a caution by the young, as a symbol of mirth and gaiety!

Fencing is an exercise of admirable utility in itself; it strengthens the body, and infuses courage; but it is applicable only in later years, and has a connexion too dangerous with what is called the point of honour. Much the same may be said of riding: suitable as it is to the manly character, we cannot begin with it before the bodily powers are almost entirely developed.

* "Can it be believed, that many parents confine their children within doors, lest the wind and sun should tan their skins? This is particularly the case with the female sex: but delicacy is not langour; and ill health is not necessary to render a woman pleasing."—EMILIUS.

We have now arrived at the end of the usual exercises admitted into the fashionable world. Every intelligent person will instantly perceive that they are next to nothing, for nothing remains at the bottom but the dance, that can be at at all times practised. If many boys of this class had not exercise, of their own selection, adapted to their natural gaiety,—and did not various circumstances occur in the process of their lives to assist the body in some sort, and to compensate in many respects, as far as they possibly can, for this effeminate education,—our men of fashion would soon be converted into women of fashion; and they would be seen only at their knitting, their drawings, or their piano-fortes. The perpetual female society (of sisters, aunts, cousins, nursery-maids, and chamber-maids) in which the boys of our people of fashion are brought up, infests like the dry-rot: they soon like the style of refinement, are startled at the sight of a spider, or any other insect; have spasms, sentiment, and vapours; and accustom themselves to such an over-anxious care of their complexion, as by no means befits a man who has his proper occupation in the state, and assuredly no time for extraordinary attention to a continually infirm body.

Nature forms all creatures with the same power, and after the same standard, in the present day as in ages past; and we must not ascribe our physical degeneracy in the least to any alteration of her laws and her energy, but to contingent causes: that is, to a defective developement of the germe, through the fault of our parents, and of circumstances, to deteriorated education, to a debilitated way of life, and sometimes to disadvantages of climate.

These contingent causes, it is true, can never force nature to annihilate her laws, and deface the mould she heretofore employed; but they may prevent the execution of her design in particular cases. If, then, the accidental impression does no more than prevent the execution of nature's design, *it can operate merely on the individual, not on the species.* It cannot fantastically change a whole race of beings, and play the scene-shifter with organized nature. Thus all the weakness of the present refined race of men is only individual weakness: and even that we term hereditary, when the weaknesses and defects of parents are entailed upon their children, is nothing but the continued operation of the accidental impression. Consequently, in proportion as these contingent causes and their operations are removed, nature will proceed to fashion man after her original rule.

But the possibility of this removal is taught us by daily experience, which frequently exhibits to us stout and strong children born of little and weak parents, thus showing that these accidental causes and their operations are very unstable.

These not unfrequent cases strongly merit the attention of the parent and the physician. While we abstain from diligent inquiry into their causes, and satisfy ourselves with the vulgar remark, " He or she takes after the grandfather, or some one or other," as a matter of course, we shall make but little progress in physical education; much less, I may say, than in the education of domestic animals, the breed of which we have often sufficient industry and intelligence to improve throughout whole countries.

We find no people upon earth exceeding us in longevity; but few in hotter climes attain the age of seventy or eighty; and the negro at forty or fifty is an old man. With what right, then, can it be pretended, that the term of our lives is decreased? Our corporal frame increases till the age of twenty, or, perhaps, twenty-four. If we would draw an inference from the analogy of plants and animals, nature seems to have established it as a law that the period of growth shall be nearly a third of that of the whole duration;

and hence the term of our existence on this planet seems limited to seventy, or, perhaps eighty, years, and if this age be attained, upon the whole, by the smaller number of us only, the fault is not in any declension of the natural powers, but, as already in the time of David, in the way of life; that is, in millions of circumstances, which tend to destroy the individual before the period allotted him by nature: some species of murder in disguise, not nature, is at the bottom. It is the same when half of all who are born and die before the age of ten.

CHAPTER II.

Consequences of the ordinary Mode of Education, particularly the Neglect of Bodily Improvement.

In the beginning of the Bible it it is said, " In the sweat of thy face thou shalt eat bread." This the multitude have looked upon as a curse—the philosopher alone perceives in it an universal medicine. I might easily mould it to my favourite notion, and quote it as the most ancient injunction of improving the body by gymnastic exercises. The expression, " in the sweat," clearly implies bodily exertion; but the spirit of hierarchy and indolence has explained it as alluding to mental labour also, probably as a shelter against the reproaches of the labouring classes. All the learned, the great, and the rich, readily approved such an explanation; and accordingly exposed themselves to the scourge of all those evil consequences, which naturally flow from neglect of this truly valuable rule of life.

Propensity to luxurious living united with indulgence in bodily rest; and from their embraces sprung an army of infirmities. Even the ancient Athenians possessed the fatal art of producing new diseases.*

Let physicians decide whether we have not exceeded them in this. Diseases unobservedly grow into fashion, as formerly witches and ghosts! by degrees they are considered as necessary and natural accompaniments of human exist-ence, and to repel them recourse is had to physic. Instead of investigating the true ground of this lamentable state, and going to work afresh, as far as circumstances would permit, men at length discovered the cause of their infirmi-ties to be their delay of employing the physician.

It is time to break off. If we figure to ourselves our unnatural way of living, screwed up to the highest pitch, to become universal but for one century, must we not tremble for the existence of the civilized part of the human species? Happily, however, this universality has never taken place, because it is impossible; and the class of people labouring in the sweat of their brows has only given to the intellectual world of the learned and the great, from time to time, strong and lusty recruits, without suffering itself to fall entirely into their way of living.

But the class of men of learning formerly, to whom the education of youth has been relinquished throughout all Europe, has done irreparable injury, by training the young vigorous shoots to their way of life, within their thick-walled solitary cells. Let some remote stranger, who knows no

* "Is it not shameful to require the aid of physic, not for wounds merely, and casual transitory diseases, but in consequence of indolent inactivity and luxurious living? Is it not shameful that men, resembling bladders filled with wind and water, should have laid the disciples of Esculapius under the necessity of inventing new names for diseases, as vapours and catarrh?"—PLATO DE REPUBLIQUE, lib. iii. Francfort, 1602, p. 622.

more of these institutions than Anacharsis, the Scythian, of the Gymnasia of the ancients, enter these domes, and he will imagine he is introduced to an assembly of human minds, compelled from their sixth year to abstract themselves from the body, in which they are allowed to remain solely because it is impossible to have them completely separate from it. When he observes the various methods employed to check every voluntary movement, he will naturally conclude, that here the body is of no estimation.

The mischief that has been done in the course of some centuries by this perverse mode of education, is inconceivable. It has been the grand source of bodily inactivity, voluptuous weakness, effeminacy, a multitude of diseases, and, in short, an innumerable portion of our sufferings. If we infringe human laws, still the consequences of this infringement may be prevented ; but if we disobey one of the supreme ordinances of Nature, on which even the durability of our complicated frame depends, we can neither shun nor diminish its effects, and our whole system will feel the shock. And surely the ordinance, " In the sweat of thy face thou shalt eat bread," is as much a law of nature as the addition, that the body shall return to the dust from which it was made. What then shall we say of a mode of education which forcibly impels us to disobey this law, by rejecting from its plan the improvements of our body with the habit of corporal exertion, and leaving these important objects to blind chance ?

The great, and men of learning by profession, have hitherto been too frequently brought up to have minds stuffed with knowledge in frail bodies—to be helpless creatures in human form. Massy palaces have been erected on sandy foundations, and in a few years the edifice has tumbled down, or become incapable of the service expected from it. Had not intellectual labour been placed to their account, as that labour which nature, the Bible, and sound sense inculcate; had they been corporally, as well as mentally improved, men of great learning would have been more healthy and vigorous, of more general talents, of ampler practical knowledge, more happy in their domestic lives, more enterprising, and more attached to their duties as men. "The man who is observant of his duty," says the worthy Ehlers, "must be a man of courage:" and are such to be found among the weak and infirm? Rousseau's words, "Strength of body, and strength of mind; the reason of a sage, and the vigour of an athlete," may sound somewhat like exaggeration on account of the ancient term employed, yet they exhibit the most perfect model of man, and the highest refinement of the mind, without improvement of the body, can never present anything more than half a human being.

CHAPTER III.

Bodily Weakness and Infirmity.

THROUGHOUT all nature, want of motion indicates weakness, corruption, inanimation, and death. Trenk, in his damp prison,* leaped about like a lion in his fetters of seventy pounds weight, in order to preserve his health; and an illustrious physician observes, "I know not which is most necessary to the support of the human frame, food or

---

* The inhabitants of the western coast of Europe require much more exercise to counteract the pernicious effects that result from the damp atmosphere, as well as to procure perspiration, than those of hotter climes.

motion." Why, then, should frank, healthy, blooming youth be fettered by the chains of a fatal system of education, confined to the house, and sparingly indulged, at the utmost, in the exercise of a walk in fair weather? Why, during bad weather, and in winter, should they be kept within doors, and as warm as if they laboured under a fever?

Assiduous occupation of the mind, and continued rest of body, will gradually destroy the strongest constitution; and especially if to these be added luxurious living. These few words display the grand outlines of our way of life, particularly in the higher classes; in short, it continually approaches more and more to the mode of living that prevails among men of letters. Thus the diseases of the study gradually insinuate themselves into the drawing-room, and still more easily into the nursery, which is too frequently converted into the student's closet. Allow me here to give a brief view of the consequences of mental exertion, accompanied with continual *rest of body*, from Tissot:

"The instrument of thought is the brain. In the exercise of thinking the delicate fibres of this viscus are in perpetual motion; they are fatigued by its continuance; and, as we all know, when urged beyond their force, they suffer an irretrievable derangement, by which all power of thinking is destroyed. All the nerves of the body originate from the brain; or I may say, with more propriety, the fibres of the brain are the first delicate roots of the nerves themselves. The nerves, therefore, must suffer, when the brain is weakened by excessive labour. Through the medium of the nerves this weakness imparts itself to the whole body, which cannot begin a single function without the aid of the nerves. Accordingly, if the operations of these be disordered, the whole economy of the bodily system is disturbed, and particularly of the stomach, which possesses many nerves of great sensibility. If, then, delicate youths be subjected to mental exertion, at a time when nature is busied in bringing the body to perfection, the consequences must be doubly injurious; for, on the one hand, nature is hindered in her endeavours to improve the body; while, on the other, the exercise of the mental faculties operates more forcibly, as at this age they require more exertion. Paratier was a man of learning in his eighth year; at eighteen he laboured under the infirmities of old age; and at twenty he was dead. Examples of a similar kind, if not equally striking, are everywhere to be found. The natural vivacity of the child and the boy is altogether unequalled. How brisk the circulation of their blood, unattainable in us unless in a state of fever! How great the vivacity of their unfettered, unclouded spirit, to which no animal mind approaches! Sweet, never-to-be-forgotten life, when pure serenity beams from the eye, when the whole machine expands in the fullest enjoyment of innocence, and truly celestial delight! This enjoyment, alas, is soon lost in the society of the serious muses, and with it the prosperity of the whole frame: this age is designed for corporal exercises, which strengthen the body, and not entirely for study, which enfeebles it, and cramps its growth."—Tissot.

The principal source of our well-being arises from the circulation of our fluids, especially the blood. A brisk circulation animates the whole man; even the phlegmatic is exhilarated, when anything sets his blood in commotion; and when this takes place in an immoderate degree, the man is agitated even to delirium. These effects are well known. Continued rest weakens the circulation, till at length the blood feebly creeps through its vessels, for the heart is not itself sufficient to give it due motion. For this, muscular movement is likewise requisite. But rest of body relaxes the muscles, diminishes the vital heat, checks perspiration, injures digestion, sickens the whole frame, and thus numberless diseases are introduced. There is not a single part of the human machine which a sedentary mode of life does not debilitate, and the nerves more especially suffer by it.

"Generally speaking," says Ackermann,[*] "a sedentary life is the source of all those diseases which physicians term cachectic, the number of which is considerable. Among them are greensickness, jaundice, atrophy, worms, tetter, obstructions of the natural excretions, dropsy, &c. &c." For these, *exercise* is the best remedy. "It strengthens the vessels," says Tissot, "preserves the fluids in a healthy state, quickens the appetite, facilitates the excretions, invigorates the spirits, and excites pleasing sensations throughout the whole nervous system."

I am far from being one of those who wish with blind enthusiasm to see civilized man converted into a wild animal, seeking health upon all fours in nature's bosom. I know that the savage has his diseases; and I believe that civilized man must be more capable of avoiding them, as he possesses more knowledge to shun their causes. Why, then, has he more? In fact, it is not civilization, but its abuse, that sinks us in this respect below the savage. Would we wish our posterity to be robust, musculous, and manly, let us first introduce these desirable qualities into our education,[†] nature will evidently prosper our endeavours, and our minds feel the benefit.

May I be indulged here in a short digression, that I may not pass over certain lamentable errors, which evidently take their origin from an effeminate mode of education, and consequent inactivity? I speak of the errors of an instinct,

---

[*] On the Diseases of the Learned.

[†] "Corpus enim male si va eat parere nequibit
     Præceptis animi, magna et præclara jubentis."
                                   Marcel. Paligen. Lib. 10.

to which unusual attention has been excited in modern days. Hence, if I mistake not, we trace them to their source. As we expect the juices of the well-nourished and tenderly-fostered hot-house plant will be earlier converted into fruit, we have every reason to apprehend the manifestation of this instinct in the subjects of our effeminate and luxurious education will be accelerated. The law, to which this instinct is subjected, remains the same now as it did in the days of Abraham, with regard to every one who is led by nature: but if we break loose from her hand, the bodily and mental constitution of the individual, as moulded by our art, takes its place, and produces at an early period, as experience shows, what nature would have longer deferred. What cannot the perpetual enjoyment of food to satiety, an artificially excited appetite, and a total ignorance of the hunger that labour creates, effect in the families of the great?

All this was not bestowed on man: he must pay for it by actual disease, or superabundance and corruption of the fluids. Miserable condition! We require but a certain proportion, never a superfluity of nourishment. If we cannot confine ourselves to this proportion, which is particularly difficult in the houses of the great, there is no other method for compensating for our excess but bodily exertion. This concocts the luxuriant juices, and diffuses them throughout the limbs, to repair the exhausted muscles. Hunger and lassitude are the pleasing consequences of sufficient bodily exercise; scarcely is the hunger appeased, when lassitude ensues, and with this instinct is stilled, as nothing stimulates it. How delightful is then the sleep of rosy-cheeked innocence! This is a grateful idea, for it embraces the infinite beneficial consequences of this state both to the body and to the mind.

IF the object of amusement be to recreate the mind or the body, or both, after labour performed, they must be useless in themselves, or in their application, when, instead of answering this object, they tend to exhaust the body or mind as much or more than the labour already undergone. Do we act in consonance with reason, then, if after serious studies, or other sedentary employments, which by degrees cramp the viscera, we recur to novels, cards, and other similar amusements, invented by folly, which exhaust and debilitate anew the tired nerves and relaxed muscles? if we seek recreation in plays, balls, and concerts? if, with the digestive faculty enfeebled, we sit down to the long meal of the festive board? I may leave the reader to pursue these questions; as I have neither time nor desire to enumerate our usual games and pastimes, and show that they are for the most part injurious in themselves, or in their application? If we take but a slight glance at them, it cannot fail to strike us how few are in use that tend to promote judicious exercise of the body. What an effeminate feature is it in the character of a nation to be continually lolling on cushions in drawing-rooms or carriages, and to play almost wholly with the mind? Is it not more suitable to its destination that we should appoint to this office its instrument, the body, and thus render this body capable of serving it in its higher duties and occupations?

This is no longer the TON. "Things are now come to such a pitch, that all (bodily) exercise is banished from genteel houses; and that, as Tissot says, 'Those various bodily movements, which the ancients considered as duties, have been so neglected within the last two or three generations, that in a few years, probably their names will occur only in dictionaries.' In every town, cards, with which our fathers were but little acquainted, chain all societies from an appointed hour in the afternoon to their chairs, in which the greater part of mankind sit fixed as statues till the night is far advanced. Even our taste for music serves but to restrain us the more from air and exercise; and, fond as I am of this celestial enjoyment, I can scarcely blame the eastern nations for deeming it indecorous in a man of rank to learn music."*

Can we, then, talk of ton, when our general improvement and perfection are in question? And why is it no longer the ton? Because our education favours effeminate inaction and sensibility, and even calls in the aid of science to play with the mind; because all its aim is to soften our feelings, and so to unstring us, that we have no desire to seek recreation except in repose and inactivity of body, and always prefer what flatters our delicate sensibility.

"Over this," says Frank, "police should have a watchful eye; this is not the way to render useful citizens of the states, after having performed their labours, apt for fresh exertions for the good of their fellow-men."

Even our children, who are yet too young, and too little departed from nature, to adopt the refinements of fashion, could teach us better. They frisk about the moment the book is closed; and sit not still, like us, preaching of decorum, till impelled by those commands of nature which we dare not disobey.

Debilitation of the Mind.

No one doubts the great influence of the body on the mind; the physical treatment of the body, therefore, particularly in childhood and in youth, must tend to determine the character of the mind, and indeed affects it more

---

* Frank's Medical Police.

deeply than is commonly supposed. This is so certain, that it may be brought to the test of experiment. Confine a young creature in a dark dungeon, treat him as a criminal, and deprive him of every youthful enjoyment; what a melancholy, gloomy, suspicious, unsocial being will he become ! keep him in religious solitude, let him fast, and pray, and mortify his flesh; he will probably become a pious enthusiast, a visionary, a fanatic. The man who climbs the mast, unfurls the sail, and guides the helm, is a very different being from him who is destined to the thimble and the shears. Our ideas of ourselves and the things around us, our way of thinking and acting, too frequently depend on the modifications of our fluids, on the tone of our nerves and our whole frame. To thousands the world appears to-day, serene and bright; to-morrow, dismal and gloomy; to-day they can displace mountains, to-morrow they cannot move a straw. This complete change of scene and action is commonly produced by the state of their bodies alone. If truth and sincerity, firmness of character, unalterable constancy in love, cheerfulness, presence of mind, courage, and true manliness of sentiment, have decreased in modern days, the fault is not in the greater cultivation of the mind, which, it is to be regretted, is but too often the improvement of the imagination, wit, and memory, to the neglect of practical understanding,—but commonly in the disregard of physical education, in the want of hardening and exercising our youth. When shall the young citizen of the world acquire that great, noble, manly character, which distinguishes itself by firmness in prosperity and adversity, by courage in danger, by generosity in succour, by patience and exertion in need, by reflection in the business of life, when he is brought up with delicacy, and, taught to rely on the support of others, is conscious of his own helplessness and debility, whence shall he derive presence of mind in danger, when he has spent his blooming years lolling on a sofa, or sitting on a form? whence cheerfulness, when his nerves are relaxed, and his whole body unbraced by his way of living? whence temperance, when we excite and strengthen his passions by luxury in eating and drinking, by sleep, and inactive repose? whence constancy, sincerity, and truth, when his constitution is weak, and represents the things that surround him now of this hue, anon of that? in a word, what can we expect from the mind, when its instrument, the body, is not only capable of executing little, but even oppresses the mind with its weight?

Destroy the root of the healthiest plants, their heads will droop and die. Many excellent qualities of the mind have their roots, in fact, in the body; their summits, which adorn the spiritual being, the mind, will wither, if we neglect the soil of these valuable plants, and thus injure their roots.

No heroic patriotism, no sacrifices for the common good and the succour of others, no manly courage, no inflexible love of truth, no lofty endeavours at noble actions, can ordinarily be expected from the weak and from persons habituated to luxury from their youth; who are ever thinking on the gratification of their sybaritic wishes, and what they call their wants; whose grand business is solely the acquisition of the means of gratifying them; and whose bodies, sunk in ease and effeminacy, seek to shun every inconvenience by a thousand devious ways. The objects of their exertions are enjoyment, pleasure, their own convenience, ease, and freedom from care; their common lot is to be slaves to their passions.

CHAPTER IV.

Inactivity.

LET us diminish sensual susceptibility, desirous only of pleasurable impressions, and endeavour to give more force to the body and to the mind. Indolence is the consequence of weakness and voluptuousness. A contented mind, in a strong body steeled by education, loves labour, and to be active. We have to contend with many passions, the grounds of which lie wholly in our corporal disability. That phlegmatic indolence, which cannot bear to stoop to pick up a handkerchief, or to undergo the intolerable exertion of a little walk to serve a fellow-creature ; which converts men into mere babblers without the power of action ; flourishes best in the bosom of effeminate, enervating education, the plan of which has been sketched by luxury and refinement. Its melancholy effects are palpable throughout the whole of this country. Essentially we are as active as nature, from whose bosom we proceeded, and of whom we are a part. The inextinguishable flame within us was kindled from that, which is all life and activity. It is innate in us. The young energies of the suckling strive to display themselves, and our third word is to enjoin the child rest. To scream, to cry, to crawl, to run, to leap, are the circumstances in which he finds satisfaction ; and we should leave him to pursue his own course as far as decorum will admit, for time and nature will convert this infantile wildness into manly, indefatigable activity. What, then, becomes of this natural activity in multitudes in their riper years ? We behold them sunk in indolence. Has nature resumed from them the gift she once bestowed ? No : not nature, but our unnatural guidance. We forcibly impose on children the manners and steadiness of maturity, and thus the inactivity of old age appears in the season of manhood. Our severity and incessant chiding still the infantile propensity to cry, and thus we gradually suppress all desire of displaying and exerting the corporal faculties, which we evidently ought to promote; we confine all labour to the mind, and by this, by improper diet, and by treating him as if sick, we weaken the activity of the future man. If his mind be not immediately affected, it will infallibly suffer by this conduct: the phlegmatic body creeps at its commands, and seldom obeys them if they be not perfectly agreeable to it.

"The weaker the body, the more it commands: the stronger it is, the more it obeys. The body must possess vigour to be obedient to the mind: a good servant should be robust."*

But without repeated exertion it will soon become weak, and vegetate in a state of insubordination. Here we are at the fountain of the worst of diseases, *idleness*, and its companion, *ennui*. At this point I shall stop, otherwise I must play the spy over the gaming-table, at which Avarice, Scandal, and Despair so frequently seat themselves; domestic quarrels, from the cottage to the palace; complaints of want of bread; and the sighs of indolence when compelled to labour: I must ask many impostors why they do not perform what they promise; many searchers after the philosopher's stone, why they do not rather follow the plough. How often shall we find that effeminacy, and the habit of bodily inaction, are at the bottom of all these?

The best education leads to the best capacity for supporting the joys and the sorrows of life.

To support requires force, and that this cannot be imbibed from the spirit of our present effeminate mode of

* Rousseau's Emilius.

education, which weakens and softens our feelings, is self-evident. If, therefore, we would approximate the best education, we must gradually abandon this spirit. Not that we must abjure learning and civilization, and with them genuine moral sentiments, but only follow those ancient principles, which lead to form and sustain the manly character by exercise and well managed hardening, instead of curtailing our natural strength and greatness of mind.

It is inconceivable how, in the long series of ages during which an acquaintance with ancient Greece and Rome has been cultivated, the excellent principles of physical education pursued in those countries, and of course the accounts of their *gymnastic exercises*, have been read and re-read in every school, and every study, without anything being introduced from them into the education of the day. But men too frequently read words only, not ideas.

" The ancients had so high an opinion of gymnastics, that Plato and Aristotle, not to mention others, considered a commonwealth as defective, in which they were neglected : and, indeed, justly ; for if the improvement of the mind ought to be our constant aim, and the mind cannot accomplish anything of worth and importance without the aid of the body, assuredly it is incumbent on us to promote the health and dexterity of the body, that it may be capable of serving the mind, and assisting, instead of impeding, its operations. For this reason Plato in Pythagoras, calls him a cripple, who, cultivating his mind alone, suffers his body to languish through sloth and inactivity."*

" There is not a greater and more reprehensible mistake in education, than the raging propensity of compelling children to extraordinary (mental) exertions, and exacting from them a rapid progress; *this is the grave both of their*

---

* Hieronymus Mercurialis de Arte Gymnastica, Amst. 1672, p. 14.

health and their talent, and notwithstanding all that has been said against it by men of great abilities, who have attacked with more force than success, it is still by far too common."*

This age, I shall repeat with Tissot, is designed for bodily exercise, which strengthens the frame, and not entirely for study, which enfeebles it and checks the growth.

O! ye parents, lay to heart this discourse in favour of innocent creatures, whom nature, relying on your affection, has delivered into your hands—who are your own flesh and blood—and who, with amiable simplicity, in a great measure, depend on you for their destiny!

" Love childhood—encourage its sports, its pleasures, its amiable instinct. Which of you has not sometimes regretted that age,—when the mouth is ever decked with smiles, and the mind continually at peace?"†

Even the innocent sports of children will promote the development of the mind, by exercising and strengthening the organs, without which the act of thinking is impracticable; and they lay the foundation of that harmony between the corporal and mental faculties, from which probably arises what we term a sound understanding. Children will remain more apt for instruction, if we do not break the spring of their capacity for it, by too early overstraining: nay, they may enjoy it perpetually, if we have but the art of intermixing it with their bodily exercises.

Ridicule.—It is true, that the singularity of Gymnastic Exercises would in some places attract notice, and might excite laughter: but if this may be deemed a sufficient reason for neglecting what our reason approves as proper to be done, we must relinquish every improvement in the least striking for its novelty.

* Tissot on the Health of Men of Letters.

† Emilius,

"Whatever people may say or do," says Stuve on this very subject, "no man of probity should suffer himself to be deterred from the direct road to a great and important end. An intelligent schoolmaster will undoubtedly encourage his scholars, both by precept and example, in every thing that respects the care of the body, from a sense of duty."

Danger.—This seems to be inseparable from Gymnastic Exercises; but long experience has convinced me that it merely seems so. For fifteen years I have been in the habit of teaching a great number of ladies and gentlemen of all ages, weak and strong, little and big, awkward and expert, daily engaged in Gymnastic Exercises, from the lowest degree to the highest and apparently perilous, and to this day not one of them has received any injury. This is a stronger argument than any reasoning upon the subject. With effeminate fears I shall not endeavour to contend: for why should I labour in vain? these may prohibit running or riding, and even eating or drinking, as they may be attended with danger. But let the timorous parent and tutor reflect, that we cannot always live in our chambers; and that a young man incurs a thousand times more danger if we send him into the world with a delicate frame, and unpractised limbs, than if we gradually form him, as far as we can, *to overcome difficulties.*

"To avoid exposing children to a few natural evils, you create for them evils which nature never intended."*

* Emilius.

CHAPTER V.

On the Use and End of Gymnastics.

THERE was a time when diseases were little known, when age was almost the only infirmity, and death the sole physician. This period was not governed by the sceptre of Saturn, as the ancients say, but by that of *nature*; when her sovereignty was no longer acknowledged, the golden age fled away, and man began to study physic. Still, however, it lingers here and there, where the son of nature, in a happy climate, reposes, after moderate labour, in the shade of the bread-fruit tree; where, blackened by the fervid heat of the solar ray, he cultivates his cassava and rice; where he pursues for miles the stag and the wild ox, or tend his peaceful herds on the banks of the Niger and the Mississippi, or on the Alpine heights.

One revolution only deserves the name of great; the *transformation* of the active son of nature into a feeble and refined animal; every other is but child's play to this. Now, after a review of two thousand years, in which the fate of mankind everywhere and at all times exhibits the same consequences of rudeness and refinement, the observer's heart sinks within him when he compares the two states together, and balances the happiness they produce. In the one scale is the *natural man*, in the fulness of bodily health, strength, and activity, with few wants, and these easily satisfied; his eye beams with the pleasure of existence—he enjoys the sense of his strength and liberty; and if anything press upon him, he has sufficient energy to resist it. Life, while it continues, is to him a source of delight: he never fancifully mounts into the region of chimeras; he has no conflict with the phantoms of a diseased imagination, and when death at length requires him to resign all the gifts of nature, no one takes his departure more cheerfully. In the other scale *is the man of refinement*, of delicate health and feeble body, with an endless series of wants. His eye too frequently expresses the bitterness of sorrow that arises from his situation; whether real or imaginary, it matters little. With him nothing goes well; the sense of his weakness torments him; he wills more than he can perform; he suffers from every pressure, and sinks under it, instead of resisting; and when death comes, he finds his wishes increased.

In these sketches there is much truth. I am no friend to Arcadian reveries; I know that the man of nature has to contend with disease, with want, and with the debility of age; but far less, and with much greater success, than his refined brother, whose actual sufferings are increased by a number of imaginary evils, and who, of feebler nerves, is much less able to repel or support them. The former almost uninterruptedly enjoys to old age that charm of life which we taste only when we are fortunate in our childhood; the latter frequently loses all enjoyment of life with his boyish years, and sinks into the arms of care and trouble. In short, *that*, possesses *bodily-well-being, with mental rudeness;* this, *infirmity and refinement, with a cultivated mind.*

I shall not here decide which of the two enjoys the greater happiness in life; but this is incontrovertible, that, if we unite in our imagination the corporal perfections of the man of nature with the cultivated intellect of the more refined inhabitant of the world, we shall have the most perfect model of the human species—a model at the contemplation of which the heart beats high.

The union of these is a problem that has long engaged the attention of men, and has been deemed at one time an impossibility, while at another it has been held very practicable. It is unquestionably one of the most important problems in which all the polished part of the human species is interested. Probably this union is not attainable to the height of perfection; but will this justify us in abandoning it altogether? Certainly not.

" Let man be cultivated as much as may be, and let his natural rudeness be polished away, but never subject him to enervating refinement."*

Harmony between the mind and body is the sole and true end of Gymnastics. This was acknowledged twenty-two centuries ago, by one of the wisest of men—by Plato.†

May I be permitted to embellish these few pages by his sentiments? They are nearly as follow :—" Many suppose that music‡ is intended to form the mind, Gymnastics the body alone. To me it appears that the mind is the sole object of both. He who pursues gymnastics only, will become hard-hearted and untractable; he who applies himself singly to music, will become soft and effeminate. But the softness of the one is the basis of a philosophical character, which, if too much encouraged, degenerates into effeminacy; if cultivated only in a due degree, becomes politeness of manners: the rudeness of the other springs from an ardent and fiery temperament, which, if properly managed, would produce courage and magnanimity; if too much heated, degenerates into harshness and barbarity. Both, therefore, should be cherished in due proportion, and then we obtain the energetic mind of a wise and manly character; otherwise we have only effeminate voluptuaries, or brutal savages. Let the man of ardent constitution give himself

* Saltzmann.

† De Republica, iii. p. 625.

‡ For many readers it may not be superfluous to remark, that the Greeks comprised under the term music the whole circle of knowledge and mental acquirements.

up entirely to music, to the delightful soothing of its gentle harmony, and dedicate his life to the voluptuous titillation of song, his natural impetuosity will be advantageously diminished at first; but if he continue the same course, his mind will grow torpid, his strength will languish, and he will enervate his whole soul. Let the same man addict himself altogether to Gymnastics, eat and exercise himself, neglect music and philosophy, his body will grow stronger, he will become bold and intrepid; but will not his mind, thus despising all intercourse with the muses, and improved by no science, no meditation, no branch of music, remain feeble and dull? Behold the foe of science and the muses! Ignorant and gross, he lives without cultivation and without manners, like a brute beast. Music and Gymnastics were bestowed on man, not for the improvement of his mind and body, (for the advantage the body derives from them is merely incidental,) but for the improvement of his mind alone, for the perfecting of his fortitude and philosophy, for the duly harmonizing of these qualities, for the strengthening or softening of them in a just degree. The artist, therefore, who combines music with gymnastics in the most eligible proportion, and applies them to the mind, is to me the most perfect musician, far beyond him who knows how to tune the strings of the lyre."

Thus far the philosophic Plato. And Rousseau must have thought much in the same manner, when he wrote:—"The grand secret of education is to contrive that the exercise of the body and that of the mind may always serve as relexations to each other."*

Let us now analyze the grand aim of Gymnastics, which no one, either before or since Plato, could possibly reprove, into its separate parts, and we shall thus have the following

* Emilius.

highly desirable qualities, that we endeavour by means of Gymnastics to attain :

1st. *Health of Body, and unclouded Serenity of Mind.*

" Nothing," said a philosopher, " absolutely nothing can indemnify us for the loss of youthful health and vigour : not wealth, not honours, not learning, not wisdom,—nay, not the most exalted virtue, not the most divine desert."

It seems altogether unnecessary to attempt to prove, that bodily motion is necessary to preserve and fortify the health. Our most celebrated physicians agree, that the sources of health are to be found in pure air, cold water, wholesome and temperate diet, and due bodily exertion. Even infirm adults become healthy and strong, when they apply to these with resolution, perseverance, and cheerfulness ; but we may seek in vain throughout the four quarters of the globe, for the means of health, if we so completely quit nature's guiding hand, and sink spiritless in the arms of luxury and ease. To this we inevitably destine our youth, and render them incapable of a voluntary resource to these fountains of health, when we accustom them to fear the weather, and restrain them from corporal exertion, which promotes all the functions of the animal machine, gives them firmness and stability, imparts strength to the muscles and ligaments, braces the nerves, renders the circulation brisk, and diffuses health and vigour over the whole frame. Every one knows this, but every one does not regard it. I will introduce my reader to one of the first physicians of Europe, to the great practitioner, Frederick Hoffman :*

" The support of the body requires not nourishment alone, but the separation of what cannot be converted into blood ;

---

* De Motee Corp. opt. Medicin.—"Bodily Exercise the best of Medicines."

and what is daily thrown off from the blood is of this kind. This, according to Sanctorius, amounts to more than is discharged by all the other emunctories. Perspiration, then, is the principal way in which this can be effected. Consequently, all the means that are capable of promoting this should be employed; and of these the most natural, and, therefore the best, are *bodily motion and exercise*. Perspiration depends on the circulation of the blood. The skin is the seat of a number of small glands, which secern from the blood the particles that are to be discharged. These particles are conveyed from the glands to the pores of the skin, through which they are expelled from the system. Care must be taken, therefore, that abundance of blood be conveyed to those glands, in order to which its circulation must be promoted. This is accomplished by means of motion, one chief use of which this is. Another is the assisting of digestion, the promotion of the appetite, the exhilaration and refreshment of body and mind. A third consists in the expulsion of pernicious humours, whence people who are accustomed to much exercise are little troubled with severe diseases, with stone, gout, ague, cachexy, dropsy, or hypochondriacism. For, to say the truth, an idle way of life, particularly where but a small portion of fluid is taken into the stomach, is the true parent of all diseases that arise from an impurity and thickness of the blood, and have obstruction of the internal parts for their basis. On the other hand, nothing in the world is a more certain and efficacious preservative, than a sufficiency of bodily motion. It excels every medicine that can be recommended for the preservation of health and prevention of diseases; and in this view may justly be called a panacea, as it not only removes the cause of disorders, but is an effectual means of strengthening the body and keeping it in a proper tone."

What I have just quoted is the substance of the sev. first paragraphs of Hoffman's work, which pretty full exhibits the important and beneficial consequences of bodily exercise. If we attain to a sufficient degree a brisk circu lation of the blood, free perspiration, and elimination of cacochymical fluids, good digestion and appetite, cheerfulnes of mind and refreshment of body, we may hold ourselves completely secure against three-fourths of the catalogue of diseases.

Besides these effects on health, I shall here touch on another operation in our machine, which is promoted by exercise. This is the secretion of animal fluids, which, derived from the blood, are modified anew by the internal vessels, and then again mingled with the blood. If the internal vessels be in part so fine, that they determine the figure of the particles of the fluids, and, consequently, so constructed that no fluid can pass them without undergoing an improvement, the fluids cannot too frequently percolate these passages. Supposing the blood to pervade the whole body when at rest twelve times in an hour, but fifteen or sixteen times when in motion, it necessarily follows, that the quantity of secretion in the liver, spleen, brain, and other parts, where such fluids are generated, must be increased in proportion. How beneficial this must be to the human frame may easily be presumed beforehand, and is clearly proved from examination of the fatal effects of obstructions in these vessels. Francis Fuller, a celebrated English physician, who had experienced the effects on himself, particularly notices one of these operations.*

He considers it as indubitable, that the more a man stirs

* Medicina Gymnastica: or a Treatise concerning the power of Exercise, with respect to the Animal Economy, and the great necessity of it in the cure of several distempers.—London, 1707, p. 24—284.

himself the more animal spirits are secreted in his brain. And though in consequence of the perspiration induced by motion, more in proportion may be lost than the overplus that is produced in the brain; yet, he is of opinion, that "the blood undergoes a beneficial change from the increased admixture; for the true animal spirits have their office to perform in the blood, before they pass off at the skin, and they are not of that fugitive make as is commonly supposed. They seem to be intended to contemporate the acrimony of the blood, embue it with a plastic quality, and may serve to execute other functions beside that of motion."

Whoever has attended to the effects of corporal exercise, and observed the great refreshment of mind and body from it, which is not easily to be accounted for by a quickened circulation alone, will see no reason to doubt the operation just mentioned, or some one similar, whether it consist in a more copious generation, effusion, or movement of the animal spirits, as they are called, or in the activity excited by motion.

So much for the effect of exercise on the fluids of the human body. On the solids, its influence is no less important. By means of the invigorated circulation of the fluids, these acquire more vitality and nutrition; for, let the animal spirits be what they may, they are in consequence distributed to the nerves in greater abundance; and the blood, which everywhere applies itself to the solids, and thus promotes their growth, will be capable of effecting this important office in a more perfect degree, when it is impelled more copiously to every part. The same accelerated circulation will disburden them of all impure juices; and thus, as Lucian observes, "Gymnastics produce people, who are as far from exhibiting an indolent, pallid lump of fat, as meagerness; who sweat away all useless flesh, and retain only what imparts force and strength. These exercises," he adds, "perform the same office to the human frame, as winnowing does to corn; the chaff and impurities are blown away, the pure grain only is left behind."*

It is easy to conceive, that, in consequence of greater increase, the expulsion of all unsound and sluggish juices, and more especially the frequent tension occurring during exercise, the solids will acquire more strength and elasticity. Whoever lies a few days in bed feels himself weak and gdddy; sitting and standing destroy the equilibrium of the solid parts, more violent exercise is necessary to preserve it.

What has just been said of the effects of Gymnastics is of general importance, being perfectly applicable to adults, though in a far greater degree to growing youth. To these the brisk circulation of all the fluids, the moderate and duly proportioned† exercise of all the limbs and muscles, are far more necessary, partly to promote the growth of all the parts of the body; more especially to prevent the muscles and limbs from growing into disuse, whence arises a stiffness of the machine, observable in many persons who enjoyed not proper exercise in their youth; and, lastly, that the growth of each limb may continue proportionate to the rest. This proportionate growth is in many respects highly conducive to health, as well as to symmetry of person. For example, to me it appears incontestable that many people have the chest too strait for the lungs, in consequence of their not having been enabled, while growing, to expand this part daily by the forcible respiration which exercise induces : while the lungs, in the meantime, continuing their proper growth, began to form cohesions, or to be compressed in a cavity too narrow for them.

* Lucian, Anach., sec. 25.

† Proportionate exercise of all the corporal faculties cannot be so perfectly obtained from any common mechanical employment, as from Gymnastics.

Hitherto, we have considered Gymnastics only as preserving and fortifying the health; but they are certainly capable of restoring it when lost, and strengthening an enfeebled body to an astonishing degree. To this they were more especially applied by the ancient Greeks; their Gymnastics, aliptes, atraliptes, and pædolribæ were at the same time physicians; and Ikkus of Tarentum, and Herodicus, are mentioned by Plato* as the inventors of Gymnastic Medicine. Their pharmacy and ætiology were very imperfect; in the whole art of physic they were far inferior to us; and yet they treated diseases with great success; for they applied themselves with extraordinary diligence to the knowledge of the symptoms of diseases, and called in the aid of corporal exercises, particularly bathing and equitation, by means of which they supplied what was wanting to them in other remedies.

Not at that period alone, but even now, it may justly be asserted, that the treatment of diseases is imperfect without these exercises; for there are cases in which it will be absolutely necessary, to recur to bodily exercise, as long as nature shall hold on her course. Diseases that depend on the solids cannot be removed, unless we set the solids in action conformably to nature. Are you rendered weak and miserable by your passions? are your nerves relaxed, and your muscles enfeebled, by continued indolence, and inactivity of body, by warm drinks, study, and the like? and would you restore yourself by means of *internal* remedies? Ridiculous! The proceeding differs little from that which has rendered you infirm; it cannot restore vigour to the solids; choose for this a method more consonant to the nature of the case: exercise the body, have recourse to the bath.

Hear what Fuller says:—"Exercise is to physic, as a bandage is to surgery, an assistance, or medium, without which many other administrations, though ever so noble,

---

* De Republica, lib iii. p. 622.

will not succeed. It is a kind of reserve; but yet of all efficacy, that the thing you must depend upon, though itself very powerful, may yet receive its *dernière puissance* from this reserve. And to this it is, that we must undoubtedly attribute the wonderful success which the ancients had in their curing with such indifferent materials, as their pharmacy afforded them."* In fact, this great physician recommends bodily exercise against consumption, a species of dropsy, and hypochondriacism.

Serenity of mind is the immediate consequence of health of body. Deprive a man of this, and he is at once impoverished, his mind is palsied; to him nature appears a wilderness; the world, a vale of tears; benevolence towards his fellow-creatures gradually vanishes from his heart; the indulgence of affection, and the welcome of cheerfulness, are strangers to him; his mind is engaged in a perpetual conflict with melancholy presentiments, and gloomy cares. With it falls the grand pillar of his health. But what is to be thought of children, of boys, of youths, in the garb of melancholy, with the forced smile betokening woe? of young men without cheerfulness, at an age when all around them should be paradise? The formation of their minds, their progress in knowledge, the moulding of their heart, and the welfare of their body, depend on gaiety and peace.

Enough! If Gymnastics produced nothing but health and cheerfulness, assuredly the practice ought to be universally adopted.

2d. *Hardiness, an Improved Direction of the Passions, and more Manly Sentiments.*

The day of our birth introduces us into the midst of dangers, the multifarious operations of the elements, of living beings, of events: we feel them incessantly, as long

* Medicina Gymnastica, p. 67—284.

as long as we exist, and it is not in our power to escape
them; it behoves us, therefore, to learn to resist them.
For this, strength and firmness of body and mind are necessary. As not our welfare merely, but our very existence
here depends on these qualities, they are undoubtedly the
most important that man can possess. Man was created
in his present situation by the Deity himself; and can it be
supposed, that he should not possess from nature the
capacity for a stability necessary to maintain him in it?
Everything that destroys this capacity is called enervation;
what is it that enervates us? It is softening sensuality,
usually called by the gentler name of refined manners,
which overruns the soil of Europe with Oriental luxu-
riance.

Every creature strives after what is pleasing to it. The
despot, instinct, impels the brute to seek as pleasant what
it prescribes. Here we find rigorous necessity, founded on
the structure of the animal machine, as well as on its destination; yet man tames the elephant and the beast of prey,
and teaches them tricks for amusement; yet he feeds the
eagle, the seamew, and the stork with bread alone; the
cow, with dried fish: he binds instinct in the chains of habit.
Habit, therefore, is paramount to instinct. In man, instinct
has little force; everything that is pleasing to him is rendered so by habit.

A young Esquimaux, remote from Labrador, eats roast
beef at an English table; but with what raptures did he
behold a seal cut up! I knew a boy who used to slide
barefoot on the ice. A person having compassion upon him,
gave him a pair of shoes; but when he wanted to slide he
pulled them off. Think of a man in boots lined with fur!
Hence we may deduce the following consequences :—

What is pleasing depends merely on habit, and the
modification of our senses is entirely its work. Accordingly,

it is neither barbarous nor severe, to accustom the young citizen of the world, who has yet no habits, to any thing we please, however repugnant it may be to our feelings, which have acquired an opposite bias.

Parents, it is your duty to take upon you the guidance of your children's senses, and to conduct them uniformly in that direction which leads to manliness and strength of mind and body. Gymnastics unquestionably afford no slight means of approaching this end more nearly than has hitherto been done. They lead the pupil to exercise, where he steels his muscles, integuments, and nerves; where bodily fatigue of various kinds becomes pleasant to him; where he acquires what we term manliness; where, in short, he is more inured to receive from the hand of Providence the troubles of life with manly patience and activity, because he has not merely learned to endure, but to feel pleasure in exercising his powers in endurance.

Thus man appears in a great and amiable point of view. Not so when he is early enfeebled by an enervating system of education.

It is scarcely credible how far the body may be rendered proof against all weathers, and against even violent exertions, by daily exercise; hear what the celebrated Gruner says:

"The Gymnastics of the ancients deserve to be sedulously studied, and introduced with suitable alterations. I am persuaded they would prove an excellent means of rendering our men and women, youth and maidens, boys and girls, whom sentimentality has enervated, once more healthy, strong, and hardy."

Is it not possible again to bring strength of nerves, and manliness of mind, as much in vogue as weak nerves and sentimentality have been for years the fashionable disease?

3d. *Strength and Address, Courage and Presence of Mind in Danger.*

That these qualities may be promoted by Gymnastics, needs no proof. It is a truth so generally acknowledged, that it is commonly supposed to be the sole end of Gymnastic Exercises. Difficulties and dangers depend on an infinitely diversified combination of circumstances, and in consequence are infinitely varied, so that we can take account only of the most common : but every exercise must be generally valuable, which contributes in any way to form the body, though we are not able to discern how it may prove serviceable hereafter against this or that particular danger.

If we confine youth too much during the period of their growth : the time when nature is labouring to develope their different limbs in due proportion : we treat them improperly ; and if we counteract Nature's efforts by too much sitting and repose, or by immoderate exertion, how shall their bodies retain their symmetry ?

Both extremes must and will be avoided in a good education. This takes care that youth do not sit too much : it gives strength and elasticity to all the muscles by moderate exertion ; it invigorates the growth, and promotes the symmetry of the body by a regular circulation of the fluids ; it imparts to the physiognomy openness and gaiety, somewhat of manliness and courage, with a slight tint of pleasing dignity and an enterprising spirit.

All this is in a great degree attainable, if not in every instance completely, by the daily use of pleasing exercises begun in early childhood ; nay, very perceptible progress towards it may be made, even if we have let slip the first six years. A word or two, however, by way of explanation. It is easy to be conceived, that every limb must acquire increase of strength and bulk through exercise ; for this impels the fluids more forcibly into it; so that the muscles are visibly rendered turgid: and if these fluids, the blood more especially, contain those particles which promote the growth of the limb, they will, of course, deposit a greater abundance of nutritious particles in the limb that is exercised, and enlarge its substance. Every one may try this experiment on himself; let him take hold of a rope, and draw himself up from the ground by means of his hands; let him throw a stone twenty times with all his force, or the like, and the enlargement of the muscles of his arms will become visible to his eyes. Hence may be deduced the rule: would you have the legs strong? run and jump frequently; and so of the rest. As to the physiognomy, it appears to me sufficiently determined that it is produced partly by the long-continued operation of the internal feelings, partly by the occupations of the body. Thus the sorrowful features of vexation and disappointed hope, or the rugged distortions of despair, gradually impress themselves on the countenance of him who has long been a prey to suffering; and thus the physiognomy of the tailor commonly differs from that of the blacksmith; the countenance of the man of letters from that of the soldier.

Innocence, unconstrained cheerfulness and activity, are the most excellent sculptors of the human countenance. Gymnastic exercises are preferable to them all; and if they promote temperate exertions, firmness, and courage, they will season the innocent, serene, and lively physiognomy with the features of manly decision and fearlesness, and thus confine the expression of gay pleasing innocence with energetic fortitude.

4th. Mental Beauty.

Our morality depends on the will, and this is entirely governed by the views of our minds. This is unquestionably true; yet here no connexion between morality and bodily perfection is apparent. But the best views, and the best will, secure nothing more than the theory of good actions; they alone do not render a man truly moral and virtuous; for with both he may remain a mere moral verbalist. People of this sort, whom we would mildly term theorists, are abundantly numerous; they all say, with Paul: "To will is present with me, but how to perform I find not."

Performance requires the power of action, and to exert this power, the body is usually of prime importance; it must be strong, healthy, and adroit, before performance is practicable. Here, then, the connexion between morality and Gymnastics is clear and incontestable.

But this subject admits of other points of contemplation. Through the means of the body we acquire our perceptions and ideas; their modifications depend on it, and from them our views are derived. Thus here again there is connexion between morality and the condition of the body. On this subject much may be said. In a word, our moral health and energy are commonly the result of our physical health and strength, and our moral failings are often nothing more than consequences of our bodily defects.*

The firmness and equanimity of a man under all circumstances, his courage in defence of the truth, the magnanimity with which he encounters everything, even the elements themselves, to save a fellow-creature, his intrinsic benevolence, &c., &c., are more or less the result of his bodily health and strength. There are feeble and infirm, yet patient sufferers, of great moral energy, it is true; but we admire them precisely because they are exceptions to the general rule.

---

* "Physical decline and moral depravity are intimately connected; and those laws which are requisite for the preservation of health, serve also to preserve and improve the morals."—DOUBLET, the Physician. See Hofland's Annals of Physic in France, vol. ii. p. 395.

Lastly, if we consider Gymnastics only as an innocent mode of employing our time, as a preservative against the dangers of idleness, of how much advantage may they be in a moral view.

The complaints respecting want of amusement for youth are general, but for this we ourselves are to blame, since we commonly attend only to one branch of their activity, that of the mind; I might almost say that of the memory and imagination alone; the other, equally important, that of the body, we leave to chance; and when this introduces no occupation, we find the circle of youthful employments too contracted. In truth, if Gymnastics served only to guard youth against ennui, pernicious books, and the like; if they rendered it the prevailing fashion among youth to seek their chief pastime, and the principal delight of their leisure hours in corporal exercises, they would certainly do much.

The Greeks already had this important object in view in their Gymnastics. " Our young men are exercised," says Solon to Anacharsis, in Lucian, "partly for the purpose of rendering them valiant warriors. But then they are likewise so much the better citizens in time of peace; they do not contend in trifling things; idleness does not lead them into scandalous debauchery, they spend their leisure hours in these exercises."

I shall likewise recommend to serious consideration what Boerner says. If, with proper attention to diet, both in eating and drinking, with the due promotion of a free, tranquil, and moderately brisk circulation, " the body be diligently exercised in various ways, and fortified against the impression of soft sentiments, the boy will grow up to a youth, the youth to manhood, without pernicious and detestable propensities finding any place to take root."

5th. *Acuteness of the Senses, Truth of Feeling, and Penetration of Mind.*

At our birth we enter upon the stage of the world almost insensible. Our organs are perfect, but our capacity of perfection is still asleep. Impressions from without awaken it by degrees; we learn to use our organs, to perceive with increasing facility and clearness the impressions we receive through them; and our understanding begins to exercise itself in judging of what we perceive by means of our organs.

Thus the thinking faculty of man is gradually formed through the means of the body, or through external impressions; could we keep these from it, it would lie in a profound slumber to all eternity. On the other hand it is equally true, that the development of this faculty will take place with the more quickness the more we expose it to these impressions, thereby exercising its capacity of perfection, and affording the judgment an opportunity of improving itself by means of exercise. Hence, it is evident, that the perfection of the understanding keeps pace with the expertness of the senses, or rather of the perceptive faculty. But the more we bring our body into collision with surrounding objects—that is, the more we *exercise* it, the more will its organs be sharpened, and the mental powers be roused to examine the various relations of those objects to us, and instigate their effects.

" Would you cultivate the understanding of your pupil, cultivate the powers it is to govern, exercise his body continually, render it healthy and robust, in order to make him wise and rational; let him toil, let him act, let him run, let him spout, let him be ever in motion, that he may become a man in vigour, and he will soon be so in point of reason."*

* Emilius, vol. ii.

From what has been said, it is apparent that true re____
I do not mean the hysterical slights of genius, but what w
call sound sense, is not formed independently of the body;
nay, that a well-framed and exercised body is precisely
what facilitates and assures the proper performance of the
mental functions.*

Hoffmann cured idiots by exercise; and, according to Des
Cartes, the mind depends so much on the constitution and
state of the bodily organs, that if any means of increasing
sagacity were to be found, they must necessarily be sought
in the art of physic.†

" Many obliquities of the moral sense and understanding
are at bottom nothing more than maladies and dissonances
of the organs of sense; and I am fully convinced, that a
healthy organization, and a natural distribution and
harmony of the powers, are the essential foundation of that
noble endowment, which is called sound understanding.
As a physician, I shall be pardoned, if I think I have observed, that on this account wit, genius, inflamed imagination, enthusiasm, and the like, are far more frequent in our
generation than genuine, natural sense, and rectitude of
judgment; if I consider these splendid qualities of the present day as serious symptoms of a diseased and unfortunate
irritability of mind, not as bursts of energy; and if I ven-
ture to hope that a healthier tone of mind may be expected
from the continuance of a better and more natural treatment of the physical man."‡

Let us, then, exercise the body. Without it we cannot think; it is the loom in which we weave the lovely

---

* A very remarkable instance of neglected cultivation of the body, and
imbecility of mind arising from it, may be found in the " Records of Education," by a society of practical Tutors. Wessenfels and Leipsic, 1792,
vol. ii., p. 190.

† Hoffmann, " Motion the best Medicine."

‡ Hoffmann, " Journal of Luxury and Fashion," 1792, No. 5, p. 226.

web of thought. The better it is kept in order by use, the more easy and certain will be our work, the more natural the web, and the more shall we be able to extend and enlarge it; when it is deranged, our labour will be perplexed. "A costive habit," says the president Von Kotzebue, "may extinguish divine flame of genius."

One more very important object of Gymnastics I cannot pass over here, particularly as it is in some measure connected with the preceding. It is :—

Gymnastics ensure the necessary Intermission of Mental Labour.

The mind of a man, still more of a child, is incapable of long perseverance in mental exertion. This is a generally acknowledged truth; to which I shall add one more, to the same purpose, which is less known. Young men, and those who are not advanced in years, if healthy, and of warm constitutions, are never greatly inclined to mental exertion till their bodies are to a certain degree fatigued, I do not say wholly exhausted. Till this fatigue is produced, their body has a preponderance over the mind; and in this case it is a truly natural want, which cannot easily be silenced. Each muscle requires exertion, and the whole machine strives to employ its powers. This is vulgarly called, to have no sit-still flesh : if the fatigue be once brought on, the call for bodily exertion is stilled, the mind is no longer disturbed by it, and all its labours are facilitated.

Our common mode of education pays no regard to this. Youths appear in school strengthened by sleep and food, and too frequently, alas! thrown into unnatural heat and commotion.

How is it possible to fix the attention under such circumstances? The body requires action : if this be not allowed, it will obtain it in silence, it will act upon the passions, and above all, the fiery temperament of youth will inflame the imagination. Thus attention slumbers. We are barbarous when we attempt to awaken it with the rod; we require from innocent children what is unnatural; we inflict pain on the body to prevent its action: yet activity was bestowed on it by its Creator; yet nature renovates this activity every night. The mind is soon carried away by the whirlwind of corporal energies, and lost in the realm of chimeras.

Here I shall conclude this chapter on the object of Gymnastics. I freely avow I am far from having exhausted the subject; but many, perhaps, will think me already too long. To facilitate the contemplation of them, I shall just repeat the desirable parallel between the qualities of the body and mind :—

> Health of body—serenity of mind.
> Hardiness—manliness of sentiment.
> Strength and address—presence of mind and courage.
> Activity of body—activity of mind.
> Excellence of form—mental beauty.
> Acuteness of the senses—strength of understanding.

Now let me ask, are not these objects suited to our political institutions, to our manners, and to our state of civilization? and are they not worthy the most ardent endeavours of a cultivated people?

TESTIMONIALS FROM THE FACULTY, &c.,

IN FAVOUR OF

MONSIEUR HUGUENIN'S
PECULIAR SYSTEM OF GYMNASTICS.

THE long experience and practice Monsieur H. has had in teaching that branch of Education, and the great number of certificates he possesses from the Faculty in its favour, will, he hopes, be a sufficient guarantee to those that may wish to place themselves under his care. As a proof of the patronage he has received, he begs to subjoin the names of a few of the many persons of distinction he has had the honour to instruct in London and Dublin :—The Hon. Misses Bertie Percy ; Colonel Davidson and Family ; Capt. Doyle ; the Hon. Capt. Henry Cole ; the Hon. Capt. Liddell, Aide-de-camp. The Families of the Archbishop of Cashel, of the Bishop of Derry, of the Bishop of Cork, of the Bishop of Ferns, of the Bishop of Clogher, of the Marquis of Ormond, of Lord Downes, the Earl of Clonmel, Hon. Sir E. Mostyn, Lord Alexander, of the Earl of Howth, Lord Dunlo, of Lord Muskerry, of Lord Chichester, Lord Langford, Lord Wallscourt, Sir Francis Lynch Blosse, of General Barry, of Lieut.-Col. Pelly, of Sir Henry Jervis, of Sir Compton Domville, of Baron Foster, of Lady Louisa Fetherston, of Lady Harriet Kavanagh, of Lady Colthurst, of Sir Philip Crampton, Bart., Surgeon-General to Her Majesty's Forces in Ireland ; of Sir Henry Marsh, Bart., Physician in Ordinary to Her Majesty ; late Physician-General Cheyne ; Surgeons Abraham, Colles, Cusack, Orpen, Carmichael, Benson, &c., &.

Extract from the London Medical and Surgical Journal. Lectures by Professor SAMUEL COOPER, *delivered at the University of London.*

" There is a deformity of the spine arising in young persons who are growing with great rapidity, especially in females, which does not depend upon any disorder of the bones analagous to rickets, but on the circum-stance of such individuals not exercising their muscles equally, or on their being prevented from taking the free and unconstrained position and exer-cises most agreeable to nature. Under such disadvantages, the spine be-comes deformed, without any imperfection in the texture or development of the bones, and consequently there is no ricketty disease of them. When curvature of the spine, which has arisen from such cause, is not so consi-derable, and the growth of the individual is not yet completed, the defor-mity may be removed by letting all the muscles of the trunk be daily exercised in a free, regular, and uniform manner, so as not to suffer set to be put more into action than another. It is on these principles Gymnastic fetes and manœuvres become exceedingly useful in the treat ment of deformities of the spine, which are so common in girls during growth."

" I cannot too strongly impress on the minds of parents the necessity of Gymnastic Exercises. Those who, from false or fashionable ideas, neglect to give their children the physical advantages which result from this education of the corporal powers are answerable for more than half the bodily ills which befall their offspring in after life. And if they recollect that the energies of the mind are mainly dependent on the health of the body, they may probably perceive the moral as well as the physical advantages of Gymnastics."—*James Johnson, M.D., (late Physician to William IV.,) on the Morbid Sensibility of the Stomach, page* 89.

The judicious use of Gymnastic Exercise is an efficacious means of increasing health, especially in persons whose occupations are of a sedentary character. In such individuals a considerable portion of the muscular system is allowed to remain comparatively inactive ; and, as health consists in the due activity of all organs of the body, no one of these can be neglected with impunity. It is much to be regretted that the prevailing habits of society, and even its necessary occupations, should be adverse to that healthy exertion which was one of the chief departments of education in ancient times. Gymnastics were then in great use, and have come down to us with the highest testimonies of their utility. It is with confidence that I can recommend the process of M. Huguenin. His apparatus is complete, and seems adapted to the development of every system of muscles ; while he appears to be possessed of a competent knowledge of anatomy and the exquisite skill to direct its application.

J. SUTHERLAND, M.D.

Bedford-street, Liverpool, December 26th, 1844.

I have much pleasure in bearing testimony to the beneficial effects of Gymnastic Exercises as conducted by you, in imparting tone and vigour to the muscles of the body, and thus promoting general improvement of health and figure.

ELLIS JONES, M.R.C.S.E.

Liverpool, January 9th, 1845.

I have had many opportunities of witnessing the good effect of your system of Gymnastics, and I do not hesitate in recommending it in all cases of debility of the muscular structure and in lateral curvatures of the spine. Your Portable Apparatus is invaluable, and should be in every house.

W. WRIGHT MANIFOLD, Surgeon.

Rodney-street.

I have been for the last fourteen years, both in this country as well as in Ireland, a close observer of Professor Huguenin's system of Physical Education, and I feel much pleasure in giving my testimony to its value, as being the most powerful and judicious means of inducing muscular development, corporal activity, and rude health to the rising generation of this locality, whose business habits necessarily deprive them of the usual means of taking that exercise necessary for health. I conceive the scientific arrangements adopted by this enterprising and accomplished gentleman an inestimable blessing.

JEROME SMITH, Surgeon.

Hamilton-square, Woodside, January 8th, 1845.

Entertaining the highest opinion of the Gymnastic and Kalisthenic Exercises as practised by Monsieur Huguenin, I can confidently recommend them as admirably calculated to strengthen weakly habits, and to increase the vigour and agility of the more robust frame, as well as for the removal of distortions and contractions that may have arisen from debility or disease.

CHARLES MAUL, Surgeon.

Southampton, 8th February, 1837.

I am fully satisfied that Gymnastic Exercises, as at present practised, excel all others for the purpose of increasing muscular strength, and improving the health and vigour of the body : they also, from not giving rise to contention, have the most beneficial effect on the moral disposition and temper. I have formed my opinion on this subject from considerable experience, having had a Gymnasium for the use of the medical students in Trinity College during several years, which was the first establishment of the kind in this country. I highly approve of Monsieur Huguenin's qualifications as a teacher : he is a perfect master of his art, and possesses the most extensive and well-contrived machinery for his objects. I have always admired the extreme gentleness and kindness of manner he employs in the instruction of his pupils, and I consider the influence of such an example of the greatest consequence, where a large number of young men are collected together.

JAMES MACARTNEY, M.D.,
Professor of Anatomy and Surgery in Trinity College, Dublin.

"I cannot too strongly impress on minds of parents the necessity of *Gymnastic Exercises*. Those who, from false or fashionable ideas, neglect to give their children the physical advantages which result from this education of the corporal powers, are answerable for more than half the bodily ills which befal their offspring in after life. And if they recollect that the energies of the mind are mainly dependent on health of the body, they may probably perceive the moral as well as the physical advantages of Gymnastics."—JOHNSON.

I have had the pleasure of witnessing the Gymnastic Exercises performed by Monsieur Huguenin's pupils. In my mind they are admirably calculated to strengthen weakly habits, and to increase the vigour and agility of those of more robust frame.

A. COLLES.

22, *Stephen's Green, Jan* 23, 1826.

Having witnessed the Gymnastic Exercise as conducted at Mr. Flynn's Academy, by Monsieur Huguenin, I feel confident that these exercises, provided they be so managed that the pupil shall advance in the most gradual and progressive manner, will have the effect of adding to strength and improving health. To me they appear particularly useful in all those instances of weakness and delicacy in children, where much advantage is to be derived from (if I may use the expression) carefully graduated muscular exertion. To these exercises it is no slight recommendation, that they bring into action, not one set of muscles only, but all those whose office it is to give motion to the lower limbs, the arms, and the trunk of the body. So that, when properly conducted, the Gymnastic Exercises are a valuable remedy in the treatment of weakly and delicate children. In Public Schools they are especially useful, inasmuch as they furnish an easy and excellent method of putting an end to the pernicious system of keeping children, for many successive hours, sitting over their books—a system alike hostile to mental cultivation and to bodily health.

H. MARSH, M.D.

Molesworth-street, Feb. 18, 1826.

We have had very great pleasure in witnessing the exercise of Mons. Huguenin's pupils, and are glad to have an opportunity of testifying the success with which he has taught them Gymnastics, and the great care he takes to prevent the possibility of any accident.

CHAS. EDW. H. ORPEN, M.D.
ROB. J. GRAVES, M.D.

N. Gt. George's-street, Jan. 10, 1828.

Having repeatedly witnessed the Gymnastic Exercises as conducted by Monsieur Huguenin, I have much pleasure in testifying his qualifications as a teacher of them, and the extreme gentleness and kindness of his manner to his pupils.

I am also happy to be able to offer my testimony to the beneficial effects of such exercises, under his judicious directions, on the health and personal appearance of my own son.

RICHD. P. O'REILLY.

57, *Sackville-street.*

I have witnessed the exercises practised in the Gymnasium, Great Brunswick-street, under the direction of Monsieur Huguenin, and consider them eminently calculated to develope the muscular system, to give strength and beauty to the figure, and to guard it against deformity. The Professor's knowledge of Anatomy and Physiology, the judgment which he manifests in gradually training the different muscles, and the care he has taken to perfect the apparatus employed, appear to merit the entire confidence of the public.

CHARLES BENSON, M.D.,
Professor of the Theory and Practice of Physic to the
College of Surgeons, Ireland.

34, *York-street.*

The limits of a certificate do not admit of a full detail of the advantages to be derived from Gymnastic Exercises; but, being requested to state my opinion, I do not hesitate to declare that my first conviction of their utility has been strengthened by subsequent observation of the good effects produced by those exercises on the health and personal appearance of the pupils of the Gymnasium.

Several cases of distortion, contractions, and partial weakness have been successfully treated (without doubt, few are so hopeless as not to be relieved) by appropriate exercises, skilfully directed. Thus, the Gymnastic Exercises present to us a rational and agreeable substitute for the unscientific, often cruel, mechanical apparatus which have been in use for the removal of distortions, but which too frequently increased the evil they were intended to remedy.

In the Gymnasium, the physician may find a powerful auxiliary for the removal of some chronic diseases; and I am surprised that such means, recommended by many eminent medical writers, ancient and modern, have been so long neglected.

To the studious, and those whose avocations keep them within doors during the greater part of the day, the Gymnasium may be the means of taking much exercise in a short time; and to such as are not under the above restraints, it affords opportunity of preserving their health and strength, when unfavourable weather may intercept their usual exercises.

To all the above-mentioned purposes, the Gymnasium conducted by Monsieur Huguenin is admirably adapted, on account of the variety and careful arrangement of the apparatus. And such is the attention of Monsieur Huguenin and his assistants to their pupils, that the most timid or delicate need not be under any apprehension of injury.

ROBERT BELL, M.D.

Dublin, 4th December, 1828.

I have repeatedly witnessed Monsieur Huguenin while giving instructions at his Gymnasium; and I beg to give my strongest testimony at once to the efficacy of Gymnastic Exercises, and the superior manner in which he conducts them. Monsieur Huguenin's athletic and graceful frame gives the fullest evidence of the advantage of his art; while the kindness and gentleness with which he communicates his instructions, call for my fullest acknowledgment.

H. M'CORMAC, M.D.

Belfast, 14, *Upper Arthur-street.*

Monsieur Huguenin's Gymnastic Exercises are, in our opinion, calculated to impart tone and vigour to the muscular fibre, to call forth its latent power, and to unfold and expand the entire system. To the delicate and relaxed they will give strength, and offer a corrective for ungraceful positions and attitudes of the figure, whether the result of habit, debility, or disease. The perfection of his mechanical apparatus, and the great caution with which he directs the progressive exercises of his pupils, eminently qualify him for instructing in an art in which he has certainly attained superior excellence.

JOHN WOODROOFFE, M.D., Lect. on Anat. and Surg.
WILLIAM BULLEN, M.D.
GEORGE HOWE, M.D., Surgeon, North Infirmary.

17, *South Mall, Cork, 10th Sept.,* 1831.

TO M. HUGUENIN, &c. &c.

Sir,—If my testimony to your high merits as a teacher of Gymnastics, and to the beneficial effects of such exercises on the health of your pupils, be of any weight or value, I offer you that testimony most willingly, and thank you for your polite attention to my own children, to whom your instructions have been of admirable service.

J. J. WILLIS, M.D.

2, *Coal-quay, Cork, 14th Sept.,* 1831.

I have witnessed Monsieur Huguenin's Gymnastic Exercises at his School, in Cork-street, and am of opinion that, under such judicious superintendence, they may be rendered highly useful to the youth of both sexes.

J. PITCAIRN, M.D., Surgeon.

Cork, Sept. 15, 1831.

As reference for qualification, Monsieur Huguenin begs to subjoin the opinions of the Surgeon-General and Physician-General of Ireland :—

I have seen Monsieur Huguenin perform his various Gymnastic Exercises, and have been present when his pupils were performing under his directions. The impression upon my mind is, that Monsieur Huguenin is eminently well qualified to give instructions in an art in which he peculiarly excels, and with the principles of which he seems to be perfectly acquainted.

PHILIP CRAMPTON, S.G.

Merrion-square, Jan. 23rd, 1826

Having been present more than once, when Monsieur Huguenin was engaged in instructing his pupils, I am of opinion that he is perfectly well qualified to teach the Gymnastic Art. He appears to me to evince great intelligence, skill, and caution.

J. CHEYNE, P.G.

Merrion-square, Sept. 22d, 1825.

It is with no small degree of gratification that I see the introduction of a regular system of Gymnastic Exercises into this country which, if generally adopted, would not only conduce to give strength, beauty, and grace to the upper classes of society, and to all those who are not under the necessity of using bodily labour for their support; but would also, I am convinced, tend more than any other means to prevent those forms of disease which, though so general, are esteemed a disgrace to every family that has the misfortune to be affected by them. I allude in particular to the various affections supposed to arise from a scrofulous state of constitution, transmitted from parents to their children : for instance, swelled and ulcerated glands—curvatures of the spine—distortions of the chest—and diseases of the joints.

I have the strongest evidence for believing, that in the upper classes of society, these formidable complaints are, in the great majority of instances, induced by the folly of attending almost exclusively, in the education of youth, to the improvement of mental, at the expense of the muscular powers; and I cannot place the absurdity of this mode of proceeding in fewer words than by quoting a passage of my work on scrofula, publish in 1810, with the view of proving that this disease in most cases arises from disorder of the digestive organs, and that want of due exercise is the most common cause of such derangement:—" There cannot be a doubt that the present mode of education is calculated to debilitate the frame, from the long confinement children are obliged to endure in crowded and unventilated rooms. In fact, they should never be confined to their studies more than two hours at a time; a longer period can scarcely be attended with any advantage to their progress in knowledge, as their young minds are incapable of a more continued exertion; and if they are not allowed to indulge themselves frequently in recreation and play, they will only remain in mental as well as corporal inaction." When preparing this work for the press, I examined the various public schools in this city, and universally found that scrofula prevailed amongst them, in proportion as the children were detained from exercise. The most striking instances were observed in Bethesda and St. Thomas's Parochial Schools; where the children were remarkably well attended to in every particular, except in providing (from the indispensable want of play grounds) for the means of due exercise, which is almost as necessary to their health and development as even food itself; but those who are born of delicate parents, and may be said, from original delicacy of constitution, to be disposed to scrofula, have actually no chance of enjoying health, except they form constitutions for themselves, by exercise proportioned to the enfeebled state of their muscular powers. In the public schools in question, it was found that one-fourth of their respective numbers were badly affected with scrofula, although all were subject to the examination of medical men at the time of their admission, and would have been rejected, if exhibiting any symptom of this, or any other disease. How want of due exercise acts on the constitution, in promoting these formidable complaints, has been very fully considered in the essay alluded to. But I shall close these observations, which have already extended too far, by subjoining my unqualified approbation of this system of Gymnastics, which, if generally adopted, would render the rising generation remarkable for improvement in health, strength, and personal appearance, without the sacrifice of any legitimate objects of mental education.

This system also affords the medical man a prompt and decisive mode in some morbid cases, of promoting health, by directing in a steady manner the exercise of any particular set of muscles,—for instance, those of the back, in the most common species of spinal diseases, that which is caused by weakness of the muscles upon which the erect position of the body depends. RICHARD CARMICHAEL, Surgeon.

Dublin, Sept. 20*th*, 1825.

Monsieur H. thinks he cannot conclude these few observations with anything more apposite to the subject than the sentiments of the following able and learned writers :—

"Man, in a state of civilization, does not know how much strength he possesses; how much he loses by effeminacy; nor how much he can acquire by frequent exercise. We cannot but regard with pity these indolent beings who pass their lives in idleness and effeminacy; who never exert their strength, nor exercise their powers, for fear of injuring their health, or shortening their lives. Let us therefore, in future, exert all our powers and faculties for the good of our fellow-creatures, according to our situation and circumstances; and, if necessity require, let us cheerfully earn our bread by the sweat of our brow: even then, our happiness is greater than that of thousands of our fellow-men; and the more happy we find our lot, compared with that of the unfortunate victims of luxury, the more seriously ought we to apply ourselves to fulfil our duties."—*Sturm.*

"It is known that a good physical education fortifies the body, cures many diseases, and gives to the organs a much greater aptitude to execute the movements required by our various wants; besides greater strength and extension of the faculties of the mind, greater equilibrium in the sensations, and those just ideas and elevated passions which are connected with habitual sentiment, and to the regular exercise of a much greater force."—*Cabannis Rapport du Phisique et du Moral de l'homme.*

"The first knowledge is that of self-preservation. A severe and masculine education is always the best: it is that only which forms superior men; and of this the history of every age furnishes a multitude of examples."—*Beranger Vertus de Peuple.*

"Warriors full of courage, and politicians full of craftiness, may frequently be met with; but of those men who have a great and noble character, the result of their sentiment and their strength, no one would have become famous on the earth if his moral education had not been fortified by an excellent physical one."—*Dictionnaire des Sciences Medicales.*

GYMNASTIC AND KALISTHENIC EXERCISES.

Copied from the Northern Whig, Belfast.

In our province, as journalists, we hold it to be our duty, not only to watch over the course of public events at home and abroad, but occasionally also to anticipate their march, and attempt to guide the judgment of the public with respect to matters which they are but partially, or imperfectly, acquainted with. We, therefore, feel great pleasure in calling the attention of our readers to the subject of this article. It might appear to some, that our remarks are unnecessary; but experience convinces us that those who are not habitually engaged in utilitarian or truth-seeking pursuits, require to have even the most important facts urged, again and again, on their consideration, before they will adopt or act upon them. What can be more obvious than the advantages, nay, the necessity of regular bodily exercise, for men and women, for young and old? yet how little is it understood! While some individuals immure themselves in their apartments, until they lose the inclination, and almost the power of motion; others take exercise to excess, or pursue it at improper intervals, or in an injurious direction. A small minority are hardly anywhere to be found, who cultivate their bodily power in a systematic manner, and thereby maintain every muscle and every function in their natural vigour and integrity. Yet this is what every individual should do, or at least try to do. All should know the difference between bones and muscles, as well as between nerves, veins, and arteries. They should have some little knowledge of the structure and powers of the human body, generally, as well as the means of preserving it in health and strength. Gymnastic Exercise supplies the latter, and books of anatomy and physiology the former. It is peculiarly fortunate that this exercise may be taken with or without this knowledge; yet both are surely best. To enter into a history of Gymnastics and to give a minute detail of the various exercises comprised under that term, would here be out of place; we shall, however, try to give as much of both as our time and space will permit.*

As to the origin of Gymnastics, it may be truly said, that they prevailed in every country in which the progress of pernicious luxury had not deprived the people of power and inclination for manly and athletic occupations. This defect was an evil, however, which history teaches us invariably cured itself. When nations, by excess of idleness, debauchery, and dissipation, become enervated in body as in mind, they experience precisely the same treatment as individuals do under like circumstances; they are overthrown and destroyed by the resolute and robust. Action— action of mind and body is the law of our being; and, without it, we finally sink and perish. By this compensating principle, the world is unceasingly replenished, and the withered and fruitless branches of society are perpetually cut off. Idleness and debility, whether moral or physical, thus bring their own destruction. Under exertion, on the other

* The various Encyclopædias give interesting details of the Gymnastic Art. See also the *Dictionnaire de Medicine* and the *Dictionnaire des Sciences Medicales*, under this head; and consult the works of Captain Clias, Gustavus Hamilton, &c., and the Prospectuses of Monsieur Huguenin's Establishments. There are many works on the subject in the Continental Languages, the German, French, and Danish, especially. Among these, the Treatises in the Memoirs de L'Academie des Inscription, and the works o fSaltsman, and Professors Gutsmuths and Jahn especially occur to us.

hand, is repressed by the loss of power which it occasions; and those nations who most harassed their neighbours by war and spoliation have, at length, as a necessary result of their conduct, become unable to continue their aggressions.

History affords many illustrations of the latter; but it is most to our purpose, in this place, to dwell on the former. Who, then, does not know that the Persians, in the prime of their history a martial and vigorous race, were subsequently overcome, in repeated encounters, by incredibly smaller bodies of a nation called the Greeks—that these latter, from causes already enumerated, were overwhelmed by the Romans; and that the Romans themselves, having become debauched and effeminate, were in a manner cut to pieces by the swarms of Northern Europe? All history is full of such examples. Look at the pusillanimous conduct of the degenerate descendants of those hardy ruffians, Pizarro, Ferdinando Cortez, and their followers. The records of the past, indeed, teem with such instances; and while the memory of the reader supplies him, let us urge on his attention the important fact, that whenever men cease to cultivate their power of body and mind, to an extent at least commensurate with the progress of their neighbours, they infallibly become the victims of their negligence. What, indeed, will not courage of soul and hardihood of frame enable men, whether as nations or individuals, to perform? The glorious deeds of the children of Sparta and Helvetia, and the achievements of adventurous travellers fully prove this.

All who have had an opportunity of seeing those men who dwell in what is called a state of nature, have testified to the grace, symmetry, and perfection which their frame exhibit. This is entirely owing to their habits of bodily exertion. They never pass a day without running, riding, walking, leaping, swimming, wrestling, or dancing. Each sentiment and emotion, too, has its corresponding gesture: and, unfettered by the artificial constraint of civilized life, such men acquire a port and bearing which it is almost vain to seek for among ourselves. On the tawny plains of Africa, and in the depths of the American forests, is the " *Lord of the lion heart and eagle eye*" almost alone to be met with. A few among us still lay claim to these noble attributes of our uncorrupted nature; but the servility, degradation, and inactivity of mind and body, induced too generally by the withering agency of our faulty institutions, will, so long as they continue, prevent the number from increasing. It has been said, that the statues which have descended to us from the times of ancient Greece and Rome, were mere personations of imaginary union of human perfections: but it is not so. Contemporary documents prove, that such were copies of realities; and the evidence of our senses shows the continuance of them in modern times; too rarely, indeed, but sufficiently often to show what might be done, were proper means pursued. Races of men are capable of being perfected by judicious training, just like other living things: and it is not too much to say, that every individual of our species might by it become handsome, symmetrical, vigorous, and alert. Gymnastic Exercise would constitute an important item in this training. No education in fact is complete without its introduction; and without bodily exercise, of which Gymnastics is the science, no one, young or old, need expect to maintain his health and strength. Every one is aware of the extraordinary attention which the Greeks and Romans paid to Gymnastics, the former particularly. They made it a part of the daily concerns of life; and physicians, lawgivers, priests, and philosophers, considered the science of giving vigour and beauty to the body, not less important than of filling the mind with notions of truth, virtue, and strength. Bodily exercise was recognized by the most illustrious men of those early days, as eminently calculated to preserve health and avert disease. Every physician knows its inestimable utility, and the proverb of "*Mens sana incorpore sano,*" is as old as observation itself. Hippocrates, Galen, and Plato, are long and earnest in their encomiums on Gymnastic Exercises; and, putting aside the authority of these venerable names, the limits of a volume would not permit us to cite everything which might be collected from ancient authorities in favour of it. If the opinion of these great men, then, whom we so justly look up to, be founded on nature and observation, as in truth it is, then it is most incumbent on us to act up to the precepts which they have laid down.

The different exertions which people are daily in the habit of making, without having always any particular object in view, are seldom beneficial, except to a part of the body; and although by benefitting a part we benefit all, yet it is infinitely better to go through a regular routine, which will prove useful to every part of the body, in due succession—and thus produce a frame of the greatest strength and capability. Gymnastic Exercise enables us to do this in the best possible manner; for it takes into account every muscle, joint, and function in the body, and provides for the well-being and perfection of all. Hunting, riding, walking, are beneficial in their way; but to some they are inconvenient or expensive, while many cannot afford the time. In the Gymnasium, however, every one can, at any moment he pleases, in any weather, take exercise to any extent he may require; and, if time be an object, he can take as much in an hour, or even less, as would, in any other manner, occupy a great deal of time.

It is nearly superfluous, after what has been said, to enlarge any further on the utility of Gymnastic Exercise. Taking into account the expense of erecting buildings, and providing teachers, it is more economical than any other out-of-doors exercise, while it is infinitely more efficacious. If we look around us, upon the common run of our species, what awkward, nerveless, and infirm creatures they in general are! No blame attaches to them for this—as in most cases the nature of their employment is such, that, without having recourse to Gymnastic Exercises, it is impossible for them to be otherwise. But, we would ask, whether the incessant attention to business, interspersed only by fits of repletion and excess, or of moments of rational enjoyment—few and far between—are at all calculated to maintain the frame in the soundness and vigour which it should at all times possess? Or will this be promoted by the idleness and listlessness, to say nothing of the occasional dissipation, in which no small portion of our young people are occasionally plunged?

We have hitherto spoken of the utility of Gymnastic Exercises to men alone; and we had intended before this to enlarge on the expediency of their introduction as a branch of female education. We can, however, do little more than repeat what has been stated on this head by others; and we need not be urgent in recommending them, as they have already been introduced into every seminary of note in the three capitals of the empire —Kalisthenics is the name which the scientific cultivation of bodily strength in young women obtains. Beauty, health, and grace, are altogether inconsistent with awkwardness, deformity, and weakness; and to produce the first with certainty, it is only necessary to train with care, so far as their inferior strength will render proper, those powers which the fairer portion of our species possess in common with ourselves. Evil consequences will ensue from neglect, in the one case as much as the other; for, it is quite evident, that if those bodily faculties, whose performance is as necessary to the preservation of health in females as in men, be suffered to languish in inaction, disease and wretchedness must inevitably result. It would be impossible for us here, or in a hundred times the space, to enlarge on all the evils which excessive confinement or misdirected occupation entails on girls. It is not too much to say, that deformity, disease, and all their degrading moral consequences, are but too frequently the result. The mischievous notion is not yet quite eradicated, which condemns females, with more than Chinese barbarity, to a never-ending repetition of the most constrained demeanour of attitudes, during the whole course of their education. They should be permitted, as God and nature intended they should, to run and jump about during the whole of this, we had almost said this happy, period, (but, alas! it is not always so,) and thereby lay up a stock of enduring health for their after years. And using that discretion which common sense and rational observation suggest, nothing is more calculated to produce this desirable result than the modified system of Gymnastics, which is called Kalisthenics.

Entertaining the sentiments which we have above expressed, on the

advantage and utility of the truly noble science of Gymnastics, we c[...]
avoid expressing our satisfaction that a competent teacher of them h[...]
length arrived in Belfast; and we trust our readers will, through him[...]
preciate this art as it deserves, and thereby testify, by their approbatio[...]
the high character which our town has already obtained, in furthera[...]
and promotion of useful undertakings. We shall here close these ha[...]
and imperfect remarks by some quotations, which are all that our limit[...]
time will admit us to adduce, on the utility of the subject treated of in th[...]
paper. The world are all acquainted with the Olympic Games. W[...]
know that deification itself was often conferred on the victorious athle[...]
The legislators of old, in promoting these customs, had the design of promoting the health, and forming men to the noble office of defending their
country. Hippocrates, Galen, Boerhave, Haller, Sydenham, and the
most illustrious physicians of modern times, have passed the highest
encomiums on Gymnastics, and have indeed looked upon them as
altogether indispensable.

A recent author, distinguished in the medical science, observes, " By a
systematic exertion of the body, with very spare diet, most cases of indi-
gestion might be completely cured." And he adds, " I would recommend
some of my fair country-women, who have leisure as well as means, to
improve the languid state of their circulation, and the delicacy of their
complexion, by a system of exercise, which will give colour to their
cheeks, firmness to their muscles, tone to their nerves, and energy to their
minds."—*Dr. Johnson on Morbid Sensibility of the Stomach.*

The advantages of the training system are not confined to pedestrians
and pugilists alone, they extend to every man; and were training generally introduced instead of medicines, as an expedient for the prevention
and cure of diseases, its beneficial consequences would promote his
happiness."—*Dr. Kirchener on Long Life.*

The influence of Gymnastics on our physical, as well as on our intellectual faculties, has convinced us, after long experience and repeated observations, of the utility of the simple elementary treatise on the subject, in
executing which, we have endeavoured, as much as possible, to discard
from our lessons everything that might bear the least resemblance to the
strength and agility of rope-dancers or tumblers.

We may, however, even yet, awaken the cynic censure of the adver-
saries of every new discovery: but a very slight inspection will be sufficient to convince the unprejudiced observer, that, even in our most difficult exercises, we have not departed from our first and sole object—utility.
Far from having aimed at exciting the astonishment, or of calling forth the
admiration of the spectator, we have adopted those exercises alone which
have struck us as tending, more or less directly, to this point; whether in

developing the form, or of fortifying the constitution; whether in restoring the health, or in counteracting natural or accidental infirmities; or whether they only tend to render us more adroit in saving ourselves or our fellow-creatures from danger.

We may add, that the experience of all ages has proved beyond a doubt the salutary tendency of physical education to improve the corporal powers of man, and bring to perfection that form, which its Creator evidently intended to be the seat of perfect symmetry and beauty.

Many learned physiologists and celebrated philosophers have proceeded further in their observations, and have asserted, that the ideas of the mind become more just, grand, and capacious, in proportion to the advancement of the body in health, strength, and energy. Of the truth of this assertion, the republics of Greece and Rome afford irrefragable proofs. In these states it is notorious that physical and mental education went hand-in-hand; the most enlightened senators, successful warriors, and acute philosophers, passed much of their youth in the Gymnasium, and by its healthy exercises perfected that strength of frame, magnanimity of mind, and manliness of spirit, which proved so beneficial to their country, and crowned their own names with immortal honour. Ah! what incalculable benefit to a nation to possess subjects, thus able to fulfil all the high demands of their life and station. Such would ensure to a state a health and enterprising posterity, born with dispositions the most favourable to culture and improvement. Scions springing from a noble stock, they would resemble those vigorous grafts which only require the care of the cultivator to bring forth the most delicious and salutary fruits.

We think that indifference to the effect of a well-directed physical education can only arise from a blind attachment to custom. It seems to argue the individual born, if we may so speak, from parents whose souls were actually so absorbed in matter as to be unable to appreciate the advantages of keeping both in healthy exercise, or to comprehend the great truth—that mutual action and excitement bring mutual advantage and benefit.